To John
with best wishes

Raymond Miquel.

BUSINESS AS USUAL
THE MIQUEL WAY

Business As Usual
The Miquel Way

by

KAREN CUNNINGHAM

The Memoir Club

© Raymond Miquel 2000

First published in 2000 by
The Memoir Club
The Old School
New Road
Crook Town
Durham

British Library Cataloguing in
Publication Data.
A catalogue record for this book
is available from the
British Library.

ISBN: 1 84104 010 X

Typeset by George Wishart & Associates, Whitley Bay.
Printed by Bookcraft (Bath) Ltd.

Acknowledgements

Contents

List of Illustrations

Afore Ye Go

SET INTO A GRASSY slope at the Cherrybank building, once Arthur Bell's headquarters in Perth, stood a large, elaborate and very beautiful glass mosaic. Designed and built by the noted Scottish sculptor Sadie McLellan, it was once immaculate, the centrepiece of a spiral tiered lawn at the heart of the peaceful, attractive garden which surrounded the company's office and visitor centre. The original site now lies under an office extension built by Guinness and the mosaic itself which has been moved, sits cracked and a little forlorn, over-looking a staff car park. It was formerly serviced every year by its creator, but now its tiles are dull with weathering and lichen has begun to grow over the cement that holds them in place. The mosaic shows the crest of Arthur Bell & Sons Ltd – two red lions, supporting a shield bearing a single golden bell – and the company's Latin motto, NUNC ET SEMPER. To those among Cherrybank's thousands of visitors who have paused to admire the work, some might have wondered at the choice of motto. 'Now And Always' seems to imply a determination to resist change, and yet Bell's has, in the half-century since the arms were awarded, undergone change, upheaval and trans-formation in almost every aspect of its structure and operations. Indeed, Bell's no longer owns Cherrybank – the building was sold in 1998 to the Bank of Scotland, and the fate of this most Scottish of products is now decided, paradoxically, from an office in London. The spirit of Bell's, however, may prove a little harder to exorcise from the city.

In the first week of June 1985, when Raymond Miquel still occupied an office overlooking the gardens, Bell's was a markedly different firm from the old-fashioned distillers he had joined almost thirty years previously. Possessed and driven by a spirit of progress, it was hailed by many as one of the most successful large companies in Scotland, and the Bell's brand had become a household name, with

Miquel on the glass mosaic at Cherrybank.

22 per cent of the UK market. The cramped and gloomy workplaces he had encountered on his first visit to the company had been replaced by bright, roomy facilities and modern technology, and Bell's had expanded at an astonishing rate into a new and exciting era. As Miquel looked out over Cherrybank's immaculate gardens he knew that, with record profits of over £34 million, Bell's had successfully defied the blight which had settled on the whisky industry and left many of his competitors struggling for survival. Instead, the firm to which he had devoted most of his working life was renowned as a forward-looking company, an exacting yet progressive employer which expected much of its people but gave generously in return. Best of all, it was still an independent Scottish concern with close community ties

and an active policy in favour of sport, personal development and social welfare, reflecting Miquel's own personal priorities and beliefs. Miquel was not a complacent man; indeed, he had gone on the record as saying that if ever he felt himself getting stale at Bell's he would move on at once. But looking at the firm's healthy finances, and the ambitious expansion plans they were to make possible, 'Now And Always' was the perfect motto for both Bell's and its chairman. Both knew what they stood for; where they were going, and how they intended to get there.

'Nunc Et Semper' may be the firm's official motto, but there is an unofficial one too, far better known than the Latin. Ask any Scotch drinker and they'll tell you without hesitation – 'Afore Ye Go . . !' is as familiar as any modern jingle or catchphrase, and yet has been appearing in Bell's advertising for more than sixty years, and on millions of bottles of whisky every year. It conjures up certain images – hospitality; tradition; a civilised respite from the hurly-burly – which had characterised this fiercely Scottish firm throughout its history, and which Miquel intended to retain, however it developed in the future. The previous year Bell's had bought the Gleneagles Hotel Group in a move towards diversification, and now on the chairman's desk lay an itinerary for a sales trip to the United States, where he also hoped to clinch an acquisition which was to develop the hotels operation overseas. In short, the company was profitable and healthy, and for Raymond Miquel and his colleagues the future held no fears.

Six months later, as Miquel sat in his office for the last time, clearing his desk on a grey December afternoon, an enterprising journalist would ring and ask the outgoing chairman for one last quote 'Afore Ye Go . . !' The irony was not lost on Miquel. For years he had been identified so closely with his company that detractors derided Bell's as 'a one-man-band'. Now, watching a lifetime's work being dismantled around him by the firm's new owners, Miquel must have felt that whilst something of Arthur Bell & Son would undoubtedly survive the process, the spirit of 'Now And Always' would leave Cherrybank with him.

There were others who thought so, too. Bell's employees, each of whom received a free annual share allocation, remained staunchly committed to their board, urging him to tell Saunders; 'Awa' ye go!'

Not a single one of them sold their stake to Guinness. Neither were the media all convinced by Guinness's arguments, particularly some of the Scottish papers, for whom the spectre of closures and redundancies had a special resonance. Miquel, whose brand-building strategy favoured high-profile public relations rather than slick advertising, was a familiar figure to Scottish editors and journalists, many of whom were convinced of the special nature and achievements of Bell's and lined up to demand support for its beleaguered chairman. Likewise Scottish politicians, among them North Tayside MP Bill Walker, fought stubbornly first to preserve Bell's, and when that fight was lost, to expose the shady manoeuvring and City shortcomings that had allowed it to happen. Supporters pointed to Miquel's record and strove to convince market opinion – and the all-important shareholders – that Bell's was in safe hands. It was not to be, and although their anxieties were briefly allayed when Miquel agreed to stay on for a short period after the takeover, in an endeavour to keep its senior management in place, four months later he was gone.

The battle to keep Bell's out of the hands of Ernest Saunders and Guinness plc had proved one of the bitterest and most controversial fights in the history of Scottish business. Ten weeks of turmoil had put paid not only to an independent tradition going back a century and a half, but also to thirty years' worth of painstaking effort and dedication. If the takeover was, as many claimed, a disaster both for Bell's and for Scotland, it was also a personal tragedy for Miquel, and there was fierce speculation as to what he would do next. He had made no secret of his commitment to Scotland, or his belief that local Scottish companies and workers could, given leadership and direction, compete as equals with the best in the world. However, his individual and uncompromising approach to business had alienated many in Charlotte Square. Now there were suggestions in some quarters that Perth's marathon man might well have run his last race. Others were not so sure.

CHAPTER 1

The Formative Years

THE CITY OF PERTH has had a long and eventful history. Settlement in the area can be traced back over eight thousand years, and it was a Roman and then a Pictish town before Celtic missionaries established the first Christian community in a pleasant, fertile spot near the navigable river. Until 1482 it was the capital of Scotland, and every Scottish king until James I was crowned in Scone Abbey to the north of the town, where the Stone of Destiny was originally sited. Even after James III transferred his capital to Edinburgh, Perth remained an important centre of trade and manufacture. The town has been associated with the whisky trade since the sixteenth century, and as well as being famed for its salmon it was also once a major linen exporter, thanks to the River Tay which supplied power for the town's many mills. Perth has seen both affluence and hardship through the centuries, and when in 1825 one Thomas Sandeman opened a small wine and spirit shop in Kirkgate he must have worried that the recent downturn in the linen trade might mean few customers. Still, as a connection of the Sandemans of Oporto, a name still synonymous with the port wine trade, Thomas had certain advantages when it came to importing wines and spirits; despite the problems of the time his small business continued to afford him a fair living until his death in 1837.

By this time things were better in Perth. There was money in and around the town, and a diligent tradesman with quality goods to sell could reasonably hope for success. So it was that Sandeman's former clerk James Roy took over the business, found a new partner named Miller, and, in due course, engaged one Arthur Bell as travelling salesman. It was young Bell's job to go journeying on horseback throughout the Highlands, taking orders for the firm's goods which included not only wines and spirits but beer, tea and sundry other items. An arduous life, bearing in mind the forbidding country, poor roads and, of course, the weather, but Bell appeared to have thrived on it, and despite the twin hazards of another trade slump and the growing Scottish Temperance movement, he was able to attract sufficient orders to keep the firm in business.

Having risen within the firm himself, it is likely that Roy looked kindly on his hardworking and enthusiastic salesman, and when Miller left the partnership in 1851 it was Arthur Bell who took his place, the firm becoming Roy and Bell. Eleven years later Roy himself retired and, after an unsuccessful attempt to work in partnership with one of his nephews, Arthur Bell found himself in sole charge of the business which now bore his name.

The early years of Arthur Bell & Sons were, for the most part, a study in solid and careful progress. Bell himself was a Victorian patriarch of scrupulous rectitude and integrity and − of equal importance − he was a skilled whisky blender who valued the excellence of his product above all else. The firm's interests became concentrated more and more on the whisky trade, both at home in Scotland and overseas, but despite his determination to supply only the best, Arthur Bell was not an advertising man. He was convinced that the sheer quality of his blends would guarantee their success, and that any kind of promotion would be detrimental both financially, and in terms of the firm's respectable image. There is plenty of evidence that others tried to change his mind. Advertising was already big business, and was proving very influential on an eager and unsophisticated public. In the clamour and rough-and-tumble of this new marketplace, there were some − particularly would-be foreign agents − who complained that without branding and promotion, they simply could not convince their customers to buy Bell's products despite their undisputed quality. Bell, however, remained adamant. His salespeople took whisky direct to the customer to taste, and once tried and appreciated, repeat orders were usually forthcoming. He would not debase his blends to compete with cheap spirits, nor squander his profits on vulgar advertisements of dubious worth. Not until 1897 was the firm's first known brand registered ('Scotch Fir' Old Scotch Whisky), and even then it took until 1904, four years after Arthur's death, before the firm first labelled a bottle with the Arthur Bell & Sons brand name. By this time Bell's son Arthur Kinmond Bell −

known as A.K. – was running the company with his younger brother Robert, and he was to remain at the head of the firm until his death in 1942.

A.K., like his father before him, understood the importance of sales abroad. Arthur Bell had struggled early on to establish a sales base in London but, frustrated by a series of incompetent or dishonest agents, he had abandoned the idea and concentrated for some years on the Scottish home market and his exports further afield. This experience left him wary of appointing agents he did not know, although experiences with certain of his relatives proved that the family was not necessarily a more reliable source of trading partners. Later, however, he was to accept the necessity, and through a combination of careful research and personal recommendation a network of agents was developed throughout Britain, the Empire and further afield. As his sons grew up and entered the firm they were able to help monitor Bell's interests at home and abroad, and when they took over after his death in 1900 this hands-on, meticulous approach to sales remained a top priority.

A.K. Bell had inherited all his father's caution and business sense, and his stewardship of the company would more than justify his father's faith in him. He was, however, far more than just a safe pair of hands. A.K. had ambitions to expand, but he also had a vision of what the company stood for, and what its role in the community should be. A sportsman himself, and a believer in the benefits of exercise and fresh air, he was also a compassionate man and, like his father, felt a moral obligation toward the unfortunate and the dispossessed. Furthermore, he did not share his father's disinclination to spend, if the spending could be justified. A new headquarters in Victoria Street was acquired, and, most important of all, Bell's took over three distilleries and became not just a blender but a distiller in its own right. Between 1933 and 1936 A.K. bought first Peter Mackenzie & Co., an Edinburgh firm which owned Highland malt distilleries at Pitlochry and Dufftown, and then the Inchgower distillery at Buckie. With these purchases came premises, staff, goodwill (and useful overseas trade connections), and many thousands of gallons of high-quality stock, including some of the finest malts. Bell's market position took a leap upwards, and A.K. was not slow to capitalise on this –

judicious advertising began to raise the profile of Bell's blends, and sales confirmed the success of this bold policy of expansion.

The firm rode out the First World War, taking the unprecedented step of engaging female workers when its entire male workforce, by and large, left for France. Then, in 1920, the US voted for Prohibition, and the world whisky trade was plunged into an immediate and long-lasting depression. Even firms like Bell's, who sold little in the US, saw a knock-on effect. Profits began to slide alarmingly almost at once, and the healthy total of over £43,000 in 1922 would be a mere £11,000 only two years later. However, A.K. kept his nerve. In December 1921 the partnership was converted into a private limited company with a capital of £350,000, and the limited company of Arthur Bell & Sons was born. The following year, despite poor profits, A.K. embarked on his most ambitious community project. Moved by concern for Perth railway workers who faced unemployment and hardship in the post-war slump, he bought a parcel of land at Gannochy, near Kinnaird, and began to build a model estate. It was not an easy task; Prohibition, tariff barriers and huge duty increases hit sales and profits both at home and abroad during the Twenties and early Thirties, and in 1932 the company actually declared losses of almost £11,000. Despite everything work continued at Gannochy, and by 1932 the final house was completed. 150 modern cottages now formed a pleasant and well-planned housing estate, each occupied by a family who paid only a modest rental for their accommodation.

A.K. was much mourned, but his memorial was the threefold legacy he left his firm. Firstly: success. Despite all the problems that beset him, A.K. left Bell's far larger and more secure than it had ever been, with two working distilleries and many other important new assets. The company was no longer just a blender and merchant – it was a producer of Scotch in its own right. Secondly, he had forged a bond of affection between Bell's and Perth which would endure for many years, and which earned the company more goodwill locally than any amount of promotion could have done. And, perhaps more significant still, he had given the firm an identity. Arthur Bell had made sure his name signified quality and honesty, but thanks to his oldest son, it also came to stand for benevolence, public spirit, and a genuine concern for the well-being of others. And that was how things remained just fourteen years after his death, when a young Glaswegian picked up a copy of the *Daily Telegraph* and spotted a job advertisement which merited further investigation.

Since finishing his National Service at 21 Raymond Miquel had been employed by PE Management Consultants, who had placed him with one of their clients, a Glasgow hosiery company. Working by day and studying for a business diploma at the Royal Technical College and Glasgow Commercial College by night, the young trainee had gained a thorough grounding in the theory and practice of modern business management, and was keen to put his skills to use. His family were not poor but the war had caused them considerable upheaval – his father, a French chef, had brought them from Guernsey to London just days before the German occupation began in May 1940. During the air raids over London he would spend each night in a communal shelter in Acton and during the day visit the Chiswick Empire to watch the recordings of 'Music While You Work', as all the schools in the area were closed or on short working time. In 1941 he was evacuated to Aylesbury where he was able to attend the local school, but then in 1942 the hotel where his father worked, the Alexander Palace in Knightsbridge, was destroyed and Miquel senior moved to Glasgow to seek work. In 1943 the house in Acton was bombed and his mother decided to move the family unit to Glasgow, where the twelve-year-old Raymond began to catch up the year's schooling he had missed in bomb-damaged London, and the family established themselves in another new home. Even after the fighting was over, times remained difficult. Post-war Glasgow was scarcely an affluent city and Miquel, selling comics in the school yard or working evenings in a local snooker hall, learned to appreciate the value of every hard-earned penny.

Because of the interruptions to his education Miquel did not leave Allan Glen's School until he was nineteen, and went immediately into his National Service in the RAF. After training as a radar and wireless mechanic he was sent to RAF Kinloss to complete his two years' service. In the spartan winter conditions evenings were spent in the billet huddled around a stove, discussing with fellow airmen future life in civvy street. Graduates talked confidently of a bright future. Salary targets of ten thousand per year in five years were a common aspiration, and Miquel became aware, having no such prospects of his own, how much his future would depend on the choices he made for himself. Not that he resented his upbringing; far from it. Despite the upheavals and his father's long working hours, his had been a happy childhood, and he was particularly grateful for the education he had received. Allan Glen's was a fee-paying boys' school in Glasgow with a prestigious reputation, and it could not have been easy for his parents to find the money to send him there. They had given him the best opportunity they could, he reasoned, and it was up to him to make the most of it. He approached his two years in uniform in the same spirit and his superiors must have noticed, since Miquel's certificate of discharge, in addition to praising his keenness and co-operation, declared: 'He is above average intelligence and has a very nice manner.'

He had had vague ideas of becoming an architect, but abandoned this plan as soon as he compared the starting salary of £2.10s per week with the £6 he could earn with Production Engineering, a London-based management consultancy firm. Even this sum became unsatisfactory after a while. Miquel worked hard at his job and his evening studies at commercial college, and was an enthusiastic sportsman in his spare time, and he also loved dancing. A full social life required an income to match, and after two years he requested a meeting with his manager and explained, politely, that he felt he merited a pay rise. This strategy paid off (as it was to do again in later years), although not to the extent that he might have wished. Miquel left the office £2 per week richer, and although this was still a very modest salary by the standards of his old National Service acquaintances, it would do for the time being. He was to stay with P.E. for another two years until, looking to further his career, he applied for two jobs which both appeared to be a stepping-stone to his future. One was a management trainee post with the Co-operative Wholesale Society (CWS) in Manchester, while the other vacancy, for an 'efficiency expert', was with a Scotch whisky company called Bell's. After interviews he was offered both jobs in the same week, so the choice was either to join CWS in Manchester for £500 per year as a trainee, or Bell's for £750 per year as a work study engineer.

He chose the latter for a number of reasons. Firstly, it was in

Scotland, and Miquel already knew that his future lay in his adopted country. Secondly, it was intriguing. 'Efficiency expert' had a gratifying vagueness that hinted at all kinds of possibilities for the successful applicant. Raymond Miquel knew about work study techniques and their uses, but he knew too that these were only the beginning of the story. Furthermore, the vacancy was in one of the last industries one would expect to countenance this type of thing, let alone seek it out voluntarily. Miquel, keen and ambitious, with an excellent grounding in the fledgling science of management, had no special knowledge of what was perhaps the single most traditional industry in Scotland, but he did suspect that the job might be something of a challenge. Fortunately, that was what he was looking for.

It was not, as he freely admits, the most auspicious of beginnings. He was told later by the disgruntled finance director that he had been interviewed along with two other hopefuls by Bell's chairman and managing director, William Govan Farquharson, but had not been the first choice for the post – that individual had considered the offer for a week before declining. Nor was he the second-choice candidate, who also refused the post when it was offered. Only then did Farquharson contact Miquel again, and he must have been somewhat relieved to learn that this particular applicant was still interested in the job. Negotiations began, arrangements were made, and it was quickly agreed that Raymond Miquel, then 25 years old, would join Arthur Bell and Sons as the company's efficiency expert, based at the Leith warehouse, at a salary of £750 per annum.

The building, at 117 Whitfield Lane, Leith Walk, was typical of bonded warehouses at that time. A vast, cold, cavernous building six storeys high, with barred windows and padlocked doors, it had been bought from a bankrupt distiller by A.K. Bell in 1924 with the intention of expanding production for the export trade, and much of the original equipment remained in use thirty years later. For Miquel, the initial tour was something of a shock. He was led through what appeared to be a series of dungeons, into which a little weak daylight crept through the shutters and bars. The workers appeared quite unaware of any defect in their working environment, and the job was obviously getting done, but Miquel began rapidly to appreciate the magnitude of what he was being invited to take on. One of his most abiding memories of that tour is the visit to the bottling hall. Leith had two bottling lines, inherited from the previous owners and therefore state-of-the-art technology – in 1924. Even in the feeble glow of the building's inadequate lighting, Miquel could tell that there was much to be done. Approaching one line he found one of the girls sitting on a cushion on the floor because there was no other place for her!

His first day at work confirmed Miquel's belief that this was not going to be an easy job. Bell's had never had anyone even remotely resembling an efficiency expert before, and whilst Farquharson may have been enthusiastic about his new protégé, Farquharson was at Head Office in Perth; the Leith workforce were considerably less receptive. The manager greeted him with: 'Well, I don't know what you're going to do around here, but you can use this room if you like.' 'This room' was a little office with a desk and chair and little else. It was obvious he was the object of some suspicion. Miquel, however, assured the man he needed only a clipboard, paper and pen, which were quickly supplied. Thus equipped, he headed for the bottling hall, stopwatch in hand. Time and motion had come to Arthur Bell and Sons.

Those first months were exhausting, exhilarating, frustrating and – sometimes – rewarding. Miquel carefully timed, charted and analysed every aspect of the production process at Leith, getting a feel for how the business worked and cataloguing the bottlenecks, wastage and inefficiencies which prevented things running as they ought. He became a familiar face, and certain of the staff thawed towards the personable young man who followed them with a notepad, scribbling, clicking his stopwatch and asking polite but searching questions about how and why things were done. He was still a newcomer, though, and when it came to changing things around, supervisors and workers closed ranks at the double. Miquel had Farquharson's authority to implement new working practices, but as he was to realise, this was far from an automatic free hand.

One early incident serves to illustrate the problem. A narrow road ran all the way around the warehouse for deliveries of goods and despatches, and for efficiency's sake it seemed obvious to Miquel that a one-way traffic system should be introduced, allowing unloading and loading to take place in a logical sequence without lengthy waits or complicated manoeuvring. Directions were accordingly given, and on the appointed day Miquel retired to his office to work on his next project. His thoughts were soon interrupted by the shouts of the warehouse manager, however: 'Raymond! Come here and look at this bloody mess!' The road was entirely jammed with lorries backing and turning, some facing each other at angles, whilst others queued on the street outside to join the fray. That, growled the manager triumphantly, was what came from needless meddling! The whole episode was staged, of course, but it did bring it home to Miquel how ingrained was the resistance to change, and how very persistent he would have to be if the ideas and plans he was developing were to come to fruition.

The bottling process offered many opportunities for improvement, and one in particular caught Miquel's attention. The process of sealing the filled cartons was awkward; they were manhandled off the line by two workers and sealed by another. To get around the problem Miquel arranged for a strip of conveyor to be installed along which cartons could be rolled to a new clamp, which he had designed himself and had made by a local one-man firm, with Farquharson's permission, for the sum of £19. The clamp allowed the worker to dispense a strip of tape straight onto the carton, release the clamp with a foot pedal, then push it on its way down the line. Simple, easy and quick, and one person's task instead of three. However, when he went back to the firm for another clamp Miquel found the price had gone up to £25 – the enterprising maker had gone into production for himself, put his own brand name on Miquel's design and was busy selling the clamp to Bell's rivals!

The next two years of Raymond Miquel's life were spent running uphill, both literally and metaphorically. A typical day involved rising at five to take the workers' train to Edinburgh; a full day at the Leith warehouse, observing, planning and cajoling to get things done; back to Glasgow on the 6 p.m. train in time for night school; and a brisk ten-mile training run between 10 and 11 p.m. before bed. He was running 100 miles a week, training with Bellahouston Harriers, representing his club at road race and steeplechase competitions. It was a punishing schedule, but it worked. Within his first year he had saved the company £25,000, mainly through cutting back staffing on the overmanned bottling lines, where the only apparent reason for the number of women employed – 48 – was that it was one more than was employed by the general manager at the nearby Crabbie's bond, thus imparting some degree of superiority to the Bell's bond manager over his rival at Crabbie's. Miquel's work study techniques quickly reduced this number to 33. With concrete results like this to justify his existence, people were inclined to take him a little more seriously. Then, too, medieval working conditions in Leith were improving, with open doors and windows and a new lighting system, and the most glaring inefficiencies in the building's operations had been put right. Others were under review. It had been hard work but Miquel felt that he was winning, and this was reflected in perhaps his most extreme sporting achievement of the time. On 7 September 1957 he completed the notorious thirteen-and-a-half-mile Ben Nevis race, running up and down the mountain in a little over 2 hours 30 minutes. It was a fitting testimony to his dedication, although, as he confesses, it was anything but straightforward. 'It was really hard . . . When the mist came down at the top, you couldn't see a thing. It didn't help when they put the beads round your neck at the top to prove you'd made it to the summit, then warned you about the precipice to your right on the way down . . .' He was 16th of over 100 runners at the top but finished 50th as he kept letting other competitors lead the way in the mist. Racing blindly up and down Scotland's highest mountain may not be the ideal metaphor for Miquel's business career, but in terms of the stamina and strength he needed in his first two years with Bell's, there are certainly comparisons to be drawn. In any event, the Ben Nevis race more or less marked the end of his professional-style training regime. He would always remain fit and active, a formidable amateur sportsman in many disciplines and an enthusiastic advocate of sport and fitness for all, but after 1957 work and marriage intruded too much into his serious sporting ambitions, and with some regret he put the latter away and just continued playing tennis tournaments.

By the time he had been at Leith a year and a half Miquel had acquired a good grasp of the entire blending and bottling process, and the innovations he had introduced were attracting the attention of other senior management, in addition to Farquharson. At the time the other important figure in the company was John MacPhail, the director in charge of distillery operations and purchasing, a youngish and very influential man who was regarded by all within the industry as Farquharson's heir apparent. Much of what Miquel was doing in Leith lay within MacPhail's area of responsibility, and this had caused friction early on as MacPhail had, understandably, assumed that Miquel would be working under him. In fact, Miquel's appointment had been Farquharson's idea and the efficiency expert reported directly to the chairman and managing director himself.

Miquel did have plans, and the more time he spent looking at Bell's, the more determined he became to put them into practice, particularly his resolve to introduce management accounts to the company. The records at Bell's, although scrupulously maintained, were a practical man's nightmare, and from his first day with the company Miquel was frustrated by his inability to extract usable information from the records without hours spent ploughing through piles of ledgers, stock books and document files. His years with P.E. had taught him the value of standard costing, budgetary control and management accounts as a tool for monitoring and assessing a firm's ongoing performance, and although he was content for the moment to learn the business and do what he could with the production side, his long-term idea was to put the entire firm on a flexible, modern footing, with management accounting techniques playing a central role. He wanted to know exactly where the firm made its money; what were its most profitable lines; what were the margins on individual products. He knew there should be monthly budgets and forecasts for each function of the operation, and effective monitoring of performance. To achieve this, he would have to change many attitudes. The concept of management accounting was unknown in Bell's; neither Farquharson nor the company's current head of finance – both chartered accountants – could conceive of any system other than traditional financial accounting, and the firm's unwieldy administrative infrastructure would simply not support the kind of month-on-month reporting Miquel would have liked to introduce. Fundamental change would be needed, and to achieve this he would need to work from the company's Perth headquarters, which were still in the Victoria Street office acquired by A.K. Bell half a century previously. For the time being, though, it was Leith and the blending, bottling and distribution of Scotch which occupied his waking hours.

Though nominally a fairly junior employee Miquel achieved much in his eighteen months at Leith, and by the time he looked at the possibility of moving on, his position in the firm had been strengthened considerably. Having no line manager except for Farquharson himself, and no career structure as such, he enjoyed a kind of maverick freedom which he regarded as a positive bonus – indeed, he says, he would probably never have taken the job had conditions been otherwise. However, he had got as far as he could without straying into other areas of the operation. He needed to move on, and since it was unlikely that anyone was going to arrange it, Miquel went to Farquharson and suggested it himself. Farquharson, pleased with what his protégé had achieved so far, agreed. Miquel would move to Perth, to examine Bell's administration and see what he could do with it.

CHAPTER 2

Making an Impact

THE HEADQUARTERS BUILDING in Victoria Street, Perth, was another gloomy warren of a place. It had been bought by A.K. Bell in 1908, and at the time had been a positive step forward for the company, but now it was more than a little shabby and old-fashioned, particularly for a forward-looking firm. Its network of corridors and rooms housed the firm's administrative, sales and purchasing functions, the boardroom, and the office of W.G. Farquharson, who would now be able to keep a much closer eye on what Raymond Miquel was up to.

Farquharson, then in his late fifties, had succeeded A.K. Bell as managing director on the latter's sudden death in 1942, and had steered the firm safely through the final years of World War II and its aftermath. An old soldier himself and another keen sportsman, he had risen to a captaincy in the Royal Scots during the Great War and afterwards had trained as an accountant, joining Bell's early in 1924. When A.K. died his brother Robert had stepped temporarily into the breach, but he had always been a sleeping partner and was old and ill himself. Farquharson was the unanimous choice of Robert and the rest of the board, and took over as chairman and managing director only a month after A.K.'s death.

The war years had been difficult enough for Bell's; wartime restrictions meant that distilling was greatly reduced and eventually halted; the home market experienced rationing and stock was difficult to replace. By 1942 levels were worryingly low, and although the export market was still growing, it was increasingly difficult to maintain sales under the burden of tax, supply problems and wartime uncertainty. Farquharson had to prove himself a worthy advocate for the company almost at once, when a mammoth assessment of death duties on A.K.'s holding threatened to wipe the company out altogether. To his credit he fought off the threat, and far from going to the Exchequer, the monies from A.K.'s portion of Bell's went instead to the Gannochy Trust, which was to be the major shareholder in Bell's for many years thereafter. When distilling quotas were increased in early 1945 Bell's was among the first companies to start up the stills once more. Even then the company's future was anything but certain, but Farquharson, like A.K. before him, was not afraid of difficult decisions. Knowing how vital it was to get production back on track he invested more than £75,000 in the Blair Athol distillery, acquired by his predecessor in 1933 along with Dufftown-Glenlivet, but which had not been operational for many years. Getting Bell's third distillery running was an enormous risk; running costs would be £1000 per week, and with no payback for at least three years, but nevertheless it was done. Blair Athol was fitted out to the highest standards and reopened in 1949. In the same year Farquharson authorised an issue of £0.6 million in debenture stock, bringing new funds flowing into the cash-starved firm and setting it on course for the next chapter in its history. It was the only logical thing to do.

By the time Miquel arrived at Perth, the effects of the war on production and sales were more or less over. Duty levels during and after the war had been exorbitant, as a result of which the home market had been unprofitable and under-supplied: Bell's had sold 80% of its output overseas. By 1958 rationing was over and the domestic market was suddenly full of possibilities. The three distilleries – Dufftown-Glenlivet, Blair Athol and Inchgower – were running at capacity, and overall the business was an exciting and busy place to be. It was an ideal time for an ambitious young man to move to the heart of the company, and Miquel was hopeful that the ideas and plans he had formulated over the last two years might now get a favourable hearing.

The first Christmas in Perth saw the first major test of this arrangement. The warehouse, where one small bottling line operated, normally closed at 5.30 p.m., but as that time approached on Christmas Eve orders were still going out and it was obvious that the despatching would not be finished before the end of the day. Miquel kept staff and Excise men back an hour or so late to finish the orders, but when the building opened again on Boxing Day he was told by an angry MacPhail that he had had no authority to do so, and that such an incident must never be repeated. Miquel went to Farquharson and asked for clarification. His brief was to make the operation more efficient and do his best for the company – ought he to have sent the workforce home with work unfinished, letting down customers and leaving a backlog? What exactly was his authority? He was vindicated when Farquharson supported his actions, and an important principle was established, but there was a certain constraint in Miquel's relations with MacPhail thereafter. To his credit, John MacPhail was largely supportive of what Miquel tried to do on the production side, although he opposed any attempt to widen the latter's brief, particularly to the purchasing function, which he guarded energetically from any interference. Nor did this small victory give Miquel anything approaching carte blanche. Farquharson was developing a real regard for Miquel, but he had made it clear that the young man was not to overreach himself; 'Make haste slowly' was to be the watchword.

Not that he was afraid to come forward and make things happen. At Leith he had had to push to gain acceptance for every one of his changes, and he foresaw similar resistance – or at least inertia – in the Perth operation. It was frustrating, but he quickly learned that initiative paid off. In his first week there he was leaving the office one evening with Farquharson when the older man stumbled dangerously on the steps outside. He had asked several times for a light to be installed above the door, but had never got around to chasing the job up. Miquel promptly left him, phoned an electrician that evening and instructed him to do the job at eight the next morning, before Farquharson arrived. When the chairman wanted something done, he reasoned, it should happen immediately, and it would do no harm to be known as the person who made sure that it did.

At Perth Miquel was able to get a better overview of the company, and had the opportunity to look more closely at the product itself. Every Saturday he attended tasting sessions along with some of the other new young employees, blind-tasting various malt whiskies, and quickly discovered that he had a keen sense of taste and could usually identify the malt or grain whisky set before him. It was a profitable time, particularly since the friendly blender, one Charlie Keenan, was given to running a book on the weekly gatherings and would offer good odds if he felt confident that he could baffle his pupils with a particularly obscure dram. After a few sessions he decided to close the book as it was getting too expensive.

The blending operation was run on the same lines as in any other whisky firm, and was shrouded in mystique. The blender himself was deeply revered, a near-mythical personage whose job it was to supervise the combination of malts and grain whiskies which made up each blend, and to ensure that sufficient of each type of spirit was on hand for the job. Often a particular single malt was not available, and in this case it was up to the blender to make substitutions, using his special knowledge of whisky to ensure that the finished blend was recognisable and met the standards of the Bell's brand. It was a very skilled job, and as a result the blender wielded enormous power. To Miquel, seeking potential problems in the production process, it quickly became clear that an entire day's work could be thrown into disarray by a vanishing blender. Indeed, it frequently was − particularly on Perth race days, when up to half the office staff, including the individual in question, would be at Perth racecourse. In his early days at Leith he had seen production grind to a halt on more than one occasion because a particular malt was not available for the blend, and the blender was nowhere to be found.

Scotch whisky is matured for a minimum of three to five years before blending, and in some instances twelve years, which means that the stock-keeping function is a fairly complex one. Add to that the exacting demands of Customs and Excise, who stipulate that every drop must be accounted for, and you end up with the potential for a grand paper chase. To Raymond Miquel's mind the whisky stock control system was antiquated and in urgent need of overhaul if the blending system was to be reliable and the finished blends consistent. The problems revolved around the stock books used for recording distillery production and whisky stocks; in Bell's case, thirty or forty large hand-written ledgers in which every production run at the distilleries was recorded in chronological order and each filled cask had a separate line allocated to its history, plotting its content, strength and value. The distillery 'run' of production entered into the stock books was called a 'parcel'. When single whiskies were required for the blends at three, four, five or twelve years a cask would be taken from a 'parcel' of whisky, necessitating a recalculation of the quantity and value of each 'parcel' in the stock books at the end of the year for stocktaking and valuation purposes. This proved a mammoth task, and the finalisation of financial accounts was delayed for up to two or three months awaiting final audited stock valuations. This traditional system was common in the industry and no one ever appeared to question it, or suggest that there might be a more effective way of doing things.

Whisky stock books formed a major part of Bell's administration. They were used each day and were so heavy that they were wheeled around on trolleys, and each night they were all locked in a strong-room. At the year's end unused casks of whisky remaining on each page were taken from the stock books and listed on sheets which were then passed out to the three administration departments in Perth, i.e. financial, selling and production, so they could complete all necessary calculations to arrive at the total whisky stock valuation. Lists were split into three equal portions and when one department had completed its task the list was passed on to the next department for checking.

After seeing the operation, Bell's young 'efficiency expert' brooded hard over the system. There were three major issues to contend with. First was the availability of the required whisky when blending took place after maturation. Secondly, the cumbersome and sometimes inaccurate daily use of the stock books. Finally there was the matter of the long delays in preparing annual accounts. After much thought and planning he produced the answer, and this subject was to provide the main part of his thesis when graduating with a Diploma in Management Studies from the Colleges in Glasgow in 1962. Because there was no detailed forward planning, he reasoned, the stock function operated largely on the instincts of the blender, whose special skills were then needed to remedy the situation when, as frequently happened, certain types of whisky were not available when required. It was this state of affairs which made the blenders so powerful, at the expense of the management, whose inability to plan ahead had implications throughout the whole production and purchasing functions of the company, since a certain matured malt whisky might not be available at the blending stage if sales of blended whisky were expanding. In addition there were huge implications for quality control, since the company, in effect, relied completely on the ability of the blender to match the missing casks of whiskies in a blend to produce a consistent product. It was crisis management, and it had to go. Why, wondered Miquel, wait years before allocating the individual whiskies to a particular blend? Why should they not simply standardise and prepare the blends in writing on cards when whisky was produced at the distilleries? This would require fairly accurate forecasting of sales over a five-year period but would ensure that the correct whiskies would be available for each blend and the whiskies in the system could be updated annually dependent on the level of sales. As the majority of the 'parcels' of whisky lay dormant over the five-year period of maturation, there would be no need to recalculate all elements of stock books each year-end as part 'parcels', i.e. whiskies required for three- or four-year-old blends would be allocated on cards by blends and only used when reaching maturation for blending purposes. The relevant calculations would only be required for stock from distilleries coming into the system as it was produced, and stock being taken out for blending after the maturation period. Stock books would be eliminated.

Like all the best ideas it was simple, practical and revolutionary, and Miquel was convinced it would work. He began to make his plans, thinking through everything from the logistics of the changeover period to the master card-index system which would need to be specially manufactured. He knew there would be opposition, but regardless of this, the system was eventually introduced. At the time it required 14,000 cards in several cabinets depicting all theoretical blends of whisky. All 'parcels' of whiskies were taken from the stock books, written out on cards in blends and allocated to the card system. With the help of an audit clerk, Jimmy Whittock, who later took charge of the system, it took one year to install in 1960 as all parcels of whisky in the stockbook had to be extracted and allocated to blends. Sales in Bell's in 1959 were approximately half a million cases per year, and the number of cards required to put the system in place was manageable. In 1984 sales were of the order of 5 million cases, and introducing the system at such a time would have been almost impossible. The cardex system, specially made by Roneo, was eventually computerised and at the press of a button required blends were identified at the blending halls and each cask despatched from the appropriate distillery for blending. All blends became standard and the correct number of the required casks in each blend ensured the product was consistent in the bottle. The blender's role changed, as he was only required to check each cask when it arrived at the blending hall to ensure the quality was right. It was no longer necessary to search for a single matured whisky to match others in the blend, as blends were always complete with the required single whiskies. The system reduced annual whisky stock valuation preparations from two months to three weeks and stopped the charade of whisky stock sheets being passed from department to department. Whisky shortages were immediately identified and administration procedures were considerably simplified.

He was still studying at night school in Glasgow, and these Tuesdays and Thursdays coincided with days when he was required to work at the Leith site, so although he was now settled in Perth, a great deal of travelling was still a part of Miquel's working week. He no longer went out running every night, but remained an energetic tennis player and though he was happy enough with his energy and commitment, Farquharson was rather taken aback by the pace Miquel set himself. On one occasion, discussing growth, Miquel was reproved for his ridiculous optimism. The company's pre-tax profits for 1956 had been a little under £500,000, and Farquharson laughed indulgently at the suggestion that they might soon exceed £1m. 'Not in my lifetime!' he replied. Still, he had faith in Miquel's judgement on day-to-day matters and forgave him his moments of folly, under which heading he included the young man's unfortunate record with the sole company car, the pride and joy of Bell's accountant and company secretary, an older and rather conservative gentleman named Ian Ure who was given responsibility for looking after it.

The vehicle in question was a Zephyr Zodiac, which was generally used only by the directors. Company cars were uncommon in those days and Miquel had no vehicle of his own, so Farquharson gave him special permission to borrow it when he went to visit Bell's at Leith and to enable him to go across to Glasgow and back to Perth two nights a week for college. The company secretary, who took his responsibilities very seriously, had handed over the keys of his beloved machine with obvious reluctance, and he left the young man in no doubt that the Zephyr was a sacred trust.

Miquel loved driving, as one might expect from a man who relishes sport and competition, but the Scottish road system was relatively unsophisticated in 1957 and did not cater for the sort of speeds which appealed to him – particularly since there was no speed limit as yet. It is fortunate that the Zephyr was a large, solid machine, because in the space of six months Miquel managed to do more damage to the unfortunate car than it would actually have cost to replace it. One particularly spectacular crash occurred as he was overtaking a builders' lorry coming into Bridge of Earn on the way from Leith to an important evening meeting with Ian Ure in Perth, to discuss the introduction of management accounts. The lorry suddenly pulled out to overtake another vehicle, forcing Miquel to bounce along the hedge on the opposite side of the road, a crash which virtually removed both doors on his side of the car. Shocked but unscathed, Miquel's initial reaction was one of anger; he had already been involved in one minor accident with the Zephyr and the car had only just been repaired. He knew exactly what the company secretary's reaction would be when he saw the fresh damage, and when he saw that the offending lorry had stopped he looked forward to sharing a few choice words with the driver. Confronted with three large navvies, however, who had marched back down the road from the lorry to inspect the damage they had caused, discretion won the day. Instead of arguing with them he meekly enlisted their help to get the car back on the road and, lifting one of the Zephyr's doors onto the back seat, he continued on his way to Perth, carefully parking the stricken car outside the office with the damaged side facing away from the building.

Ian Ure was a mild man. When Miquel explained the reason for his late arrival he took the news fairly well, satisfying himself that Miquel was all right before going to inspect the damage. Together they stood at the front door and gazed at the car. 'Oh, it doesn't look too bad,' he said, with obvious relief. 'I think you'd better come round and look at the other side,' Miquel confessed. He was still rather shaken by his experience, but the sight of the damaged Zephyr sent the unfortunate

Ure into shock. They went back into the meeting, but after ten minutes or so he called a halt, too upset at the destruction wrought upon his beloved vehicle to talk business.

After this crash there was a move amongst the directors to stop Miquel using the Zephyr altogether, which would have put paid to night school since there were no trains from Glasgow to Perth late at night. He appealed to a higher court, and although Farquharson overruled the ban the incident did little to endear Miquel to the other directors, who continued to guard their own territory against him. In particular he still had little or no access to the sales, purchasing and distilling sides of the business, and whilst he had always known that it would take time to make the necessary changes, a sense of frustration was starting to creep in.

The breakthrough came unexpectedly in January 1961. Called in to speak to Farquharson, he was greeted with the news: 'Your friend MacPhail is leaving us.' Miquel was puzzled at first: he knew MacPhail, the chief executive of the cooperage firm who supplied Bell's casks, but he failed to see why his departure would cause Farquharson such obvious agitation.

'No, not him; it's our John MacPhail who's resigned. What are we going to do?'

It was an important question. Everyone in the Scotch whisky business, including Farquharson, had marked John MacPhail down as his successor and in recent years many of the company's operations, including the important distilling and purchasing functions, had been turned over to his control. An outgoing, sociable individual and a former Scottish Rugby International, he had a high profile within the industry, and as time passed and Farquharson showed no inclination to move over for the new man, MacPhail became restless. Now he had been lured away to become Managing Director of the Highland Distilleries Company, with a view to building up the then leading Scotch whisky brand in the USA, Cutty Sark, into a market force in the UK. For Miquel the opportunity presented itself and he seized it. He told Farquharson not to worry, he'd sort it out, and left the office with responsibility for both the distilleries and purchasing. In effect he had stepped straight into MacPhail's shoes, and straight into the command line below Farquharson himself. MacPhail went on to successes of his own and eventually became chairman of the Highland Distilleries Company.

To sort out the purchasing Miquel brought in David Harley, the stock-keeper from Leith who had implemented Miquel's own stock systems and knew his job inside out. Buying had traditionally been done in a vague, civilized sort of way, with no real attempt to make suppliers compete for business. Now, with Miquel overseeing the process, a proper commercial purchasing system was introduced and in the first year a saving of over £30,000 on goods purchased was achieved.

Another target was the maltings, which formed part of each distillery's production operation and which Miquel had long considered an expensive method and one lacking in quality. To make Scotch whisky one has to ferment barley, and the quality of the barley produced by the farmers has to be of the highest standard to achieve the correct yield. Bell's, like other distillers, bought its barley in small lots from many local farmers, and malting took place in a purpose-built area of each distillery. The purchasing of barley appeared to be a cosy, slightly incestuous process with the stress on maintaining friendly relations with the local farmers rather than price or quality of the crop. Since the quality of raw barley can vary enormously depending on the weather the purchasing decision was crucial, and even then the end result would depend on the vagaries of the malting process. There were too many variables altogether and Miquel had long been convinced that there was a better way.

As with blending there was a great mystique about the barley used in whisky-making and a distillery's buyer was revered for his expertise, so the first task had to be research. Miquel investigated the subject in some detail and learned to recognise barley which would deliver the quality specification required. Then he approached Bell's senior distillery manager with barley samples for inspection and was not entirely surprised to discover that the experienced man appeared to know less about them than he did. Good and indifferent samples alike were passed as 'All right'. Miquel then pointed out the problem, and revealed his plan to buy in barley ready malted from the large maltsters, and to close all the maltings at Bell's own distilleries. He met the usual horrified resistance and dire threats about the impact on the local farmers.

Ready-malted barley was a relatively new concept for the distillers, so perhaps the old guard could be forgiven for their suspicions. Maltsters had existed for years, but they had supplied the brewers, with their shorter production cycle and greater output. Quality requirements of malted barley suitable for beer are different from distillers' malt, but the new market was no problem to the maltsters, whose prices were competitive and who could, of course, be held to account for the quality of their product. Ready-malted barley promised high standards, consistent quality and better yields, and armed with his figures and arguments Miquel took the proposal to the board. Their initial reaction, it must be said, was negative, but Miquel was nothing if not persuasive and six years at Bell's had also made him extremely persistent. Stubborn resistance gave way in the face of his over-whelming arguments and the maltings were eventually closed at Inchgower, Blair Athol and Dufftown-Glenlivet distilleries. It helped that this exercise was emphatically not about labour-cost savings; malting was largely an exercise in shovelling and tended to be done by operators doubling as warehousemen. It was a victory of commercial logic, and though there were some – Miquel included – who felt a twinge of regret at the end of a tradition, the plain fact was that the new malted barley, which was produced in special 'Saladin boxes' under strict quality controls, was cheaper, better and more reliable quality than the stuff they had been producing themselves.

It is hard to comprehend the scale of the changes which took place in the production of Scotch whisky during the middle years of this century, as it transformed itself from a local craft into a global industry. For a long time the old distillery hands remembered working conditions and practices that the newer recruits found hard to believe, and Bell's was no exception. In 1964, for example, some workers at Dufftown-Glenlivet complained about the standard of the workers' lavatories and there were discussions about new toilet facilities, during which the elderly distillery manager recounted the tale of the toilets which were in his distillery in the 1930s. There were two of these, side by side in a U-shape, and the door which should have covered the front was occasionally missing. Old Tom took his paper and pipe religiously each morning to one of the units, to enjoy a leisurely read while the inevitable occurred. Unfortunately the toilets were positioned at the very end of the distillery and directly in line with the entrance to the railway station. On this particular morning Mrs McTavish was catching a train and Tom was having his usual daily break. As she passed, he doffed his cap and said, 'Good morning ma'am,' and she responded in a polite fashion. There was absolutely no need to upgrade the Dufftown toilets, joked the old man with a grin, since they were a luxury compared to the ones he'd put up with in his younger days.

Another time a new boiler was to be installed at Dufftown-Glenlivet, and the operation was carefully planned to ensure no production time was wasted. The old manager fondly recalled the boiler he had replaced at his old distillery, again back in the 1930s. Distilleries were set up as communities at that time, with housing estates for the workers and a school for their children, and the railway ran close by – there were few good roads and not many cars. The arrival of the boiler by train was a major event in the village, and it took a whole week to take it from the station and install it in the distillery. Everyone took a week's holiday during this period; even the school closed and flags flew from every vantage point. When the boiler itself arrived it was drawn from the station through the village by horses and everyone came out in force to cheer it on its way. 'What a difference today,' he told Miquel. 'You want the boiler installed and running within 24 hours.' Reflecting on the manager's stories, Miquel couldn't help feeling there was something serene and a little romantic about those good old days.

The changes continued. In 1962 yeast for fermentation purposes was delivered regularly to all Bell's distilleries from a supplier in England but it deteriorated rapidly in transit and often arrived in poor condition or unusable. Miquel decided to explore the possibility of using a large refrigerated container unit to keep the yeast fresh. He had recently met John Russell, a young man who received two lorries from his father as a 21st birthday present to start his own transport business. They discussed the purchase of the largest container unit on the market at that time and Miquel insisted that young John should paint it out in Bell's livery. He reluctantly agreed and Miquel had solved the yeast problem and taken his first step in marketing Bell's

With Sir Alec Douglas-Home in front of the 40-foot Bell's trailer.

products. A 40-foot trailer was ordered and painted with the Bell's Scotch Whisky logo and a very large bottle of Bell's. The huge moving billboard was the first of its kind on the road as no one else in the industry was using trailers in this way at the time, so it proved to be a great novelty and attracted much attention on its constant journeyings to and from the distilleries and down into England.

Even though so much was changing, Arthur Bell and Sons Ltd still had a touch of the Victorian about it, particularly when it came to public benefaction. In 1962 the firm decided to make a gift to the City of Edinburgh in recognition of the time it had operated at Leith. This took the form of the handsome Bell Tower, which was built in front of the Usher Hall in one of the main thoroughfares of the city. It bears a plaque, suitably inscribed, and has four chiming bells at the top, with a clock face on each of its four sides. It is a lasting monument to the company's connection with Edinburgh.

After John MacPhail left the company it was not long before he asked the Bell's UK sales manager to join him to sell Cutty Sark in the UK, and in September 1962 after both departures Farquharson decided to appoint four new directors; Raymond Miquel as production director; Ian Ure, the company's accountant; the Leith Sales Office manager, and the London sales manager, who was appointed as Sales Director. They joined Farquharson, Willie Miller and non-executive director Tommy Duncanson, who was a lawyer and a trustee of the Gannochy Trust, which had been the majority shareholder in the firm since A.K.'s death. For Miquel, a director at only 31, the appointment justified every ounce of the considerable effort he had invested in his career and finally laid to rest the speculations of the young national servicemen in their cold billet a little over ten years before.

By now Miquel had worked his way through Bell's entire production process from beginning to end, and had made enormous inroads into the company's administrative systems. Although he continued to monitor these functions and introduce improvements, his focus had moved elsewhere. Farquharson may have dismissed the idea of £1m profits per year but for Miquel it seemed a perfectly reasonable target, particularly now the production side had been streamlined and modernised. He longed to get into the sales division and see what could be done with it.

Farquharson's attitude to sales had been shaped largely by external events. He had taken over the dual role of chairman and managing director at the height of the war, and for most of his twenty years in office the company had been affected by wartime restrictions and their repercussions, where demand for the product far outstripped supply and the major problem was one of building up depleted stocks to cater for future years' blending needs. In effect, he had traded in a seller's market for so long that he found it difficult to consider selling in any other light; Miquel was once taken aback to see a letter from him, brusquely informing a persistent would-be customer that Bell's had no whisky to sell him and that was the end of the matter! However, the situation was different now, and an aggressive stance was needed if one was to succeed in the newly competitive, expanding marketplace.

The new sales director, Willie Geddes by name, was a popular, larger-than-life individual who talked a pretty good game. He maintained a high profile, which was said to be important for the company, and attended all the usual lunches, meetings and special events which were a feature of sales management in the licensed trade. Friendly with Farquharson, who regularly accompanied him to these events, he nonetheless had little impact on sales and proved difficult to pin down when there were important matters to discuss. After several years of increasingly erratic behaviour he left the company, and subsequently it became clear that he had personal problems which made the whisky trade a less-than-ideal working environment for him. Once again Farquharson was left in the lurch, and once again Miquel filled the gap by the simple process of suggesting that he should do so. He was given responsibility for Home Sales, and immediately embarked on a complete review of the operation, leaving buyer David Harley to take care of purchasing and Gerry Gardner as Production Manager. Gardner, two years Miquel's junior, had taken the same night-school diploma and the two men had become friends and tennis partners. When Miquel joined Bell's Gardner had successfully applied for his old job at PE, and in 1958 followed him to Bell's. Now he took responsibility for the distilleries and the blending and bottling of whisky.

The first Home Sales meeting he called was an interesting experience for Miquel. Five salesmen covered the entire country at that point and he brought them all together to introduce himself, discuss their work and explain his thoughts for the future. He was met with a chorus of dissatisfaction and negative comment, the gist of which was how difficult it was to compete with the opposition, and how out-of-touch they felt the firm was with the marketplace. For two hours Miquel listened and learned, at the end of which he announced a new rule: competitors' brand names would not be mentioned in future sales meetings. Then he went out on the road with one or two of the reps, and wryly recalls his first foray 'down South'.

'We were in Yorkshire; Bradford. I asked Don Barber the salesman to take me round all his customers, and for three hours we trailed round pubs and off-licences without a glimpse of a single Bell's label. I kept saying, 'Come on, Don, show me some Bell's', and he'd say, 'Right, come with me!', and we'd arrive at another public house and still no Bell's. Finally he turned round and said; 'OK, you want Bell's, I'll show you Bell's.' He took me up this little alley to a large hut which turned out to be the local British Legion club; he had to sign me in at the door. We went through into the next room, he marched me up to the bar and pointed to a single bottle on a shelf at the back. 'There,' he announced. 'Bell's.' I stared at this bottle and thought, if this is typical of Bell's distribution in England, the future looks good!' Miquel had come to believe firmly in team spirit and motivation as the key to success, and these salesmen showed little sign of either. Little wonder that progress in sales had been so hard to achieve.

The sales route is probably the easiest way to get into a firm, and the hardest to follow through. For every 'natural' salesman there is another struggling to meet his quota, and even where the firm is an established business with a good product its salesmen are engaged in a permanent battle of wits with suspicious buyers, crafty competitors and an image which dismisses them as commission-hungry crooks. Almost a century earlier Arthur Bell had despaired of finding an honest London agent for his whiskies, and the company had never in its history made a concerted effort to develop a good British sales force and train it to sell Bell's throughout the UK. It was good, trained salesmen the firm needed, however, if the firm was ever to become a major player in the market, and Miquel set out to recruit people with the aptitude to sell. That was not his only criterion, though: he also wanted salespeople who were prepared to learn.

In order to fill the post of English Sales Manager he approached PA Selection, who shortlisted a number of likely candidates, and Miquel arranged to spend a morning in their London offices interviewing. The first interview was scheduled for 8.30 a.m., and when Miquel arrived a little early he was asked to wait in Reception until the room was ready. He was joined by a pleasant young man, obviously the first interviewee, and the two waited quietly for a few minutes until the receptionist told Miquel that he could now go upstairs. The young man, obviously under the impression that Miquel was a competitor, wished him a friendly 'All the best!' as he left. He was more than a little thrown five minutes later to find himself facing his 'opponent' across a desk in the interview room. The young man's name was Tony Derry. He got the job, and would stay with Miquel and Bell's for almost twenty years, eventually rising to board level as the company's sales director and implementing the policies and training that made Bell's sales team the most successful in the Scotch whisky business.

Miquel's attitude to sales can be summed up by one anecdote he loves to tell. Tony Derry was involved with a tasting at Binns department store in Manchester one Christmas, and told Miquel about the difficult customer he had had to deal with. The man tried the various blends on offer, coming back several times to taste Bell's Twelve-Year-Old, but then went on over to the counter and in a loud voice, so that Derry could hear, said: 'A bottle of Chivas Regal Twelve, please.' Unfortunately the bottle slipped out of its wrapping paper as he carried it from the store and smashed on the floor. The customer began remonstrating with the shopkeeper, who refused to replace the bottle, and as he stormed past Tony Derry the latter couldn't resist the temptation to say: 'If you had purchased Bell's, sir, I would have replaced it.' Miquel, however, pointed out that it was a lost selling opportunity. 'What he should have done was to stop the guy and say: "I saw what happened. I can't give you Bell's Twelve, but I can give you a bottle of Extra Special because it's Christmas." That man would have gone away and told all his friends what a pig he'd been and what a wonderful company Bell's was. He and his friends would have sung our praises for life, and probably bought the brand too. That was a selling opportunity waiting to be taken.'

In 1963 Bell's profits had broken the £1m barrier, further bolstering Miquel's reputation and providing him with a strong bargaining point in his efforts to expand and upgrade the operation. Farquharson retained responsibility for exports, but in almost every other area of the company Miquel had established his authority to make changes and he continued to do so.

One improvement he introduced in the early sixties concerned bottle caps, which were a long-standing nuisance on the production line. Each bottle size required an appropriate cap, so for each bottling run on the lines at Leith and Perth it was necessary to change over the cap and reset the machine on the line. The different caps required

separate storage and inventory and unit costs were high, particularly
on the less popular sizes where order quantities were relatively small.
Miquel's solution was to standardise the cap sizes, first putting the
same size cap on the pint size as on the quart. This enabled the
company to make savings on purchasing by buying substantially larger
quantities of one size. The bottles had to be changed to allow this, but
once in place the measure was so successful that it was extended to the
quarter-bottle size too. There was one unexpected benefit – the new-
style pint and quarter bottles looked much more substantial with their
larger caps, and were thus more attractive to customers than their
competitors' products. Sales rose and the chairman expressed his
satisfaction with the new arrangements, although he did ask, only half-
joking, whether Miquel intended to try and put quart caps onto the
whisky miniature range next. He didn't – but the change had not
gone unnoticed in the trade. Just like the new blending system and the
closing of maltings at distilleries, this innovation was swiftly adopted.
Within a few years all the major brands had put a standard quart cap
size on their pint and quarter bottles and Bell's brief visual advantage
was gone, but in the meantime the new caps had contributed
measurably to the steady increase in Bell's market share and this
innovation remains in the industry today.

The cap episode had brought home to Miquel the differences
between the sizes of bottle the company sold, and had kindled interest
in the performance of each different line. It was, however, impossible
to make any kind of detailed financial analysis of the profit
contribution of each size, because the firm still lacked a management
accounts standard costing and budgetary control system. For example,
there was a universal acknowledgement in the whisky industry that
miniature bottles made the company little if any profit and they were
regarded almost as a necessary evil. However, there was no way of
working out the contribution per unit until 1965, when Miquel
finally achieved his long-held ambition and introduced management
accounts into Arthur Bell & Sons Ltd. He appointed a firm of
management consultants, PA, to help, and they provided a financial
consultant named Geoff Duane to help introduce the system, and
throughout 1964 he set up the systems needed and assembled and
recorded the first year's raw data. It was an enormous undertaking,

particularly since many in the company still failed to grasp the purpose and function of what was being done and were not particularly co-operative. The results, however, justified all the time and effort involved. 'When we did that first budget and produced product costs with profit contribution for all the various products, it was a revelation. We sat up all night preparing them and going through projections and we didn't realise how late it was until we looked out of the window and saw it was light.' One of the first pieces of information to come out of the product costs was the news that far from being a loss-leader, whisky miniatures were actually Bell's single most profitable product. 'It seems incredible now that we didn't even suspect this basic fact about our business until we got our first set of figures. From that day on, we had secured our financial control information.'

Management accounts, used properly, hold up a mirror to a company. Work study techniques had identified inefficiencies at an operational level, but now Bell's board could look at each of the company's cost centres individually and monitor their performance on a month-by-month basis. It made it impossible to ignore certain problems, and one in particular demanded immediate attention. For forty years all Bell's whisky output had been bottled and packed in-house on the firm's three small bottling lines, one in Perth and the two which Miquel had inspected on his first visit to Leith back in 1956. They had seen some improvements over the years, but the growth in sales meant they were no longer adequate for the company's needs. The solution was obvious, and Raymond Miquel sat down with a pad and pencil and began to sketch out a plan for a new blending and bottling plant, and to consider where it might be built. It is typical of the Miquel approach that he drew up the plans himself. He has always taken pleasure in designing and creating practical things, from pieces of production equipment through to his own home, and during his time at Bell's the company would become recognised for its creative marketing initiatives, many of which originated on Miquel's desk. He recognises and welcomes this quality in himself, despite the fact that it gives further ammunition to those who portray him as an obsessive controller. It makes one curious as to what he would have made of architecture, had he not rejected that career on financial grounds. His instincts for order, vision and design have perforce been channelled into business, where he has erected structures that defy convention but which work efficiently nonetheless, and which are as much a focus of controversy as their unrepentant creator.

Once he had a workable plan he took it to Farquharson, but the cautious Scot was unconvinced. Profits and home sales might be up, but the kind of investment Miquel was suggesting would leave the company heavily exposed, and even with a new UK sales force he saw no guarantee that Bell's output would merit the capacity of an industrial-scale operation of the type proposed. He found all manner of flaws in the plans, queried the position of everything from the production lines to the staff toilets, and passed the papers back to Miquel with praise for his efforts and a regretful shake of the head. Miquel, however, had anticipated this. He thanked Farquharson for his suggestions, went back to his office, redrew the plans and presented them again the next morning incorporating all the new requirements. Farquharson found more problems. Miquel eliminated them and politely presented a new draft.

The game went on for six months, but the result was inevitable. Finally even Farquharson had to concede that the factory on paper was a model of its kind, and incorporated everything the company could possibly need to blend and bottle quantities of whisky in the most effective fashion possible. The only question was where it might go, and that was to provide another sticking point.

Farquharson had insisted he wanted a site close to an airport and to a main road for easy access for transport, and near a railway station. The water supply also had to be acceptable. Miquel realised these were all delaying tactics; however, he was determined to find the ideal site. There was nothing in Perth that came close to the specification and in any event, Dewar's had already tied up the majority of the available workforce. He and Farquharson visited what seemed to be all the fields in Scotland until finally, leaning over a five-barred gate overlooking a 40-acre site at Broxburn, adjacent to the A8 which was then the main Edinburgh to Glasgow link road, Miquel pointed to the Pentland Hills for water supplies, the Edinburgh-Glasgow rail link as a train thundered by, and a low-flying plane coming in to land at Turnhouse airport. All requirements had been satisfied and the 'war' had been won. Construction work began in the summer of 1966 and the building – Bell's £1 million East Mains blending and bottling complex – was officially opened by Sir Alec Douglas-Home in April 1968.

Bottling production had begun at the new plant in 1967 and by 1969 the second phase of construction was complete and all blending and coopering operations moved to the site. East Mains marked a milestone in Bell's history, not only because it permitted a fast and enormous increase in production capacity, but also because of the operational methods employed, which could have had implications for the Scotch whisky industry as a whole. The traditional method of blending whisky involved the physical manhandling of casks of whisky, brought from the distilleries to the blending halls and emptied into large vats with the other whiskies which made up the categories, i.e. Highland Malt, Lowland Malt, Islay Malt and Grain whiskies. These were then pumped into the blending vats by proportion of category required to make up the standard blend. After blending, the standard blend would be returned to casks, which were manhandled to a storage area and left to 'marry' for three to four weeks. The casks would then be returned to the bottling vats to be bottled on the production lines. Each time a cask was emptied it was required to be rolled over and checked by the customs officers to ensure the last drop of whisky had passed through the bung hole.

The process was labour-intensive, inefficient, required a great deal of space and the wear and tear on the barrels was increased. Each cask, once emptied, had to be passed to the cooperage for repairs. At East Mains Miquel devised a solution which cut down considerably on manpower and space and brought the process into the twentieth century. When the casks had been brought from the distilleries and placed in vats and the blending process was complete, the standard blend was pumped through a series of pipes to casks which were stored in situ and were never moved, for the marrying process. After the three- to four-week marrying period the contents were removed by a special standpipe designed by Miquel, with a spring-loaded base to ensure the last drop of whisky was removed without moving the casks. The contents were pumped to the standard blend bottling vats ready to be bottled. It took some time to have the system approved by

Sir Alec Douglas-Home is shown the specially designed spring loaded
standpipe during the official opening at East Mains.

Customs and Excise but after many demonstrations they agreed the
casks could be drained completely. This method required several
hundred casks for the marrying process, but the entire blending
operation at Bell's could now be handled by six men and the space
required was less than half that required for the traditional method.
The cooperage costs were also reduced substantially as the rolling of
casks around the blending hall after the initial receipt from distilleries
was virtually eliminated.

Meantime at the three distilleries extra stills were installed doubling
production, so that by 1970 the annual output was approximately two
million gallons, up from 400,000 ten years previously and still
growing.

To continue his progress in the company Miquel wanted official
confirmation of the major role he was now playing in Bell's, and
whilst he had no wish to oust Farquharson, he needed greater
executive status. To force the issue he began in 1964 to look around

for another job and was soon made aware of a promising vacancy with one of the company's larger rivals. William Grant & Sons Ltd, the independent whisky company famous for its Grant's and Glenfiddich Scotch whiskies, was looking for a general manager. The company was run by two dynamic young brothers, Charlie and Sandy Grant-Gordon, as joint managing directors, while their uncle Eric Roberts was non-executive chairman. Grant's was substantially bigger that Bell's in 1964 and the position appealed to Miquel, although his heart was set on developing Bell's if he gained the status to achieve his objectives. To force Farquharson's hand he had to be offered the Grant's position. After three interviews only a handful of candidates remained in the running, and at the final discussions on a Saturday morning Miquel advised Eric Roberts and the two brothers that he intended to put an ultimatum to Farquharson − who was well known to all three − on the Monday morning, and needed to know whether or not he would be offered the Grants job. If so, and Farquharson refused to budge, then he would come to Grant's. Eric Roberts would only say this: 'There is a horse running at Cheltenham this afternoon called Arkle, who is 1−7 on to win. You have as much chance of getting this job as he has of winning.' Armed with this encouraging information Miquel delivered his ultimatum on the Monday and Farquharson agreed to appoint him deputy managing director of Bell's.

His next target was the company's exports, which had been static for years despite an expanding market. Bell's total export sales in continental Europe in 1966 came to 20,000 cases, which in Miquel's view represented a fraction of the company's potential, but although Farquharson had handed over many of his responsibilities he clung on determinedly to exports and continued to make regular trips abroad. 'He enjoyed the travel,' explains Miquel ruefully. 'He hated the idea of giving it up.' Farquharson's overseas trips were stately affairs, made where possible by cruise liner, on which he was frequently accompanied by his wife. A charming habit of his on these trips was to drop messages in bottles into the water and many were eventually posted back to Perth by their lucky finders, who were sent a bottle of whisky in return. However, this hardly constituted an export drive. The expanding company needed to shake up its approach to overseas markets if it was to keep its competitive edge and Miquel kept up pressure on Farquharson to relent. Matters came to a head that year at an angry board meeting, when after much wrangling Farquharson finally growled: 'Right – you are so damned clever, you can have Europe for 1967.'

It was the chance Miquel had been waiting for, and he quickly began to put together an export team. He already had a European sales manager: one Peter Allan, a slightly eccentric character, fluent in German, whom Miquel remembers with great affection. Allan, an ex-Colditz prisoner of war who escaped three times but was recaptured on each occasion by the Germans, had joined the company in 1964. It was important that the 1967 figures should show a substantial increase and he appointed two further European sales executives to help with this task. When the European sales for 1967 were reported they showed sales of over 100,000 cases; a fivefold increase on the previous year and evidence, if any were needed, that the potential was there in the export market and needed to be tapped without delay. Miquel believed the figures justified his request for executive authority over the entire company, but this meant more than Farquharson's giving him access to the rest of the export sales function. He wanted the post of managing director, with Farquharson remaining as chairman. Having seen the success in Europe Farquharson capitulated and appointed Miquel managing director of Bell's in 1968, at the age of 37.

There is an entertaining postscript to the export sales episode and its aftermath. One of the major problems Miquel had encountered when he took on European sales was that the Bell's brand could not be sold in France. This stemmed from a disastrous episode in 1964, when Farquharson had sent Peter Allan's predecessor out to meet Bell's French agent, an astute lady named Madame Rouyet-Guillet. This individual, Edwards by name, had been vetted and recruited for Bell's by the Management Selection agency and this was his first assignment. Farquharson had expressed great confidence that his new whiz-kid, a man of enormous personal charm, would do great things for Bell's sales abroad.

Mme Rouyet-Guillet, whose family firm had its own branded cognac, was seventy years old and a classic *grande dame*, immaculate and chic. She seemed impressed by the personable young Edwards, who immediately took her out to dinner at the Lido to discuss business. It was unfortunate that he proved to have left his wallet in the hotel, leaving his guest to pay the bill, but she accepted his embarrassed apologies and, in fact, trusted him with a loan of several thousand francs and her car as he told her he had to drive to Switzerland that night. Edwards vanished with both, to the rage of Mme Rouyet-Guillet and the intense mortification of Farquharson, who had to send Interpol after his disappearing salesman. Management Selection were equally remorseful and the replacement they found, Peter Allan, proved an excellent choice, but Mme Rouyet-Guillet held Farquharson personally responsible for the fiasco and refused to have any dealings with him at all. Since her firm had registered the Bell's name as a trademark in France at the start of the 20th century, she refused to allow Bell's to continue to use the name on the bottle. This dashed any hopes of establishing a healthy export trade to that country as the label had perforce to read 'Arthur Bell'.

After Miquel took over as MD he wrote to Mme Rouyet-Guillet in suitably penitent terms, explaining the difficulties her stand was causing the company and asking for a new start. Her reply was cautiously welcoming, but she demanded assurances that Farquharson was truly no longer managing Bell's before she would consent even to a meeting. Miquel and Peter Allan eventually went out to Paris and attended a meeting in her penthouse flat above her offices where, after long discussions, Miquel was a little unnerved to find himself smilingly summoned into the bedroom by the good lady 'for a quiet chat'. He perched carefully on the edge of the bed, wondering what was coming next, but in the event Madame proved quite serious about the chat. A friendly financial compromise was quickly reached and the Bell's name restored in the French market.

As the export division grew Miquel recruited more people, one of whom made a lasting impression. The Edwards fiasco had left Miquel inclined to trust his own judgement about people rather than that of an agency, and when he interviewed an intelligent, smartly dressed individual in his late thirties named Denis Churchill Miquel decided to take a chance, despite the man's history. Teachers, his previous employer, had apparently found Churchill something of a handful and the two had swiftly parted company, but he was obviously an achiever and Miquel was confident he could find a useful outlet for his energies in Bell's export team.

Churchill turned out to be an outstanding salesman and an absolute charmer. He was bright, accomplished, musical, spoke several languages and no challenge appeared too great for him, so Miquel turned him loose on Malta, where a paltry 200 cases a year were sold by the local agent. Churchill promptly convinced the man to try and sell 200 cases a month, a target which he achieved. Impressed, Miquel set his new salesman a project. Bell's was far and away the major brand the company sold, but they did have a few secondary brands, notably Mackenzie, and Miquel wanted to appoint agents in each country for these, treating them as completely separate from the Bell's brand. Previous attempts had got nowhere, but Churchill quickly secured agents in virtually every country in Europe, much to the irritation of the other Europe executives. The same happened in Japan, which had relaxed its trade barriers a couple of years previously but where Bell's had failed so far to find an agent. Churchill came up with no less than four potential agents in the country for the Bell's brand, one of whom was successfully appointed.

Despite his undoubted talents Churchill was not the easiest of employees. Even when he was in the country he was impossible to pin down, racing in and out of the Perth office like a tornado, blithely missing meetings with Miquel as he chased leads for his next big project. In his spare time, such as it was, he played rugby or went up to the local aerodrome in pursuit of his greatest ambition, a private pilot's licence, and it was this which eventually brought about his downfall with the company. He broke his leg playing rugby and spent four weeks off work. Returning to Perth one Monday in typical noisy, whirlwind fashion, he requested an urgent meeting with the MD. This was arranged for Tuesday morning; however, passing him in the lobby that sunny Monday evening Miquel was surprised to see him carrying his bags and asked him where he was going. 'To the airport!' was his reply. This was totally unacceptable as he had not yet had his briefing from Miquel, until he explained it was not Edinburgh airport but Scone aerodrome, a few miles up the road from Perth. Dropping his bags, Churchill proudly showed Miquel the coveted pilot's licence he had obtained while he was on sick leave, and explained his great idea of obtaining a plane, painting 'Bell's Scotch Whisky' down either side of the fuselage and flying out to his appointments in the Middle East.

Miquel told Churchill firmly that this was entirely out of the question, but the man was irrepressible. Some weeks later the company secretary, Ian Ure, who was an extremely upright and decent man, came to Miquel with a letter from a distressed local bartender whose 18-year-old daughter Churchill had taken up for a flight and then allegedly seduced. Worse was to come. Picking up the *Daily Express* a few weeks later, Miquel found himself reading a front-page story about the dramatic rescue of a Japanese woman off the coast at Brighton. She had apparently walked into the sea in an attempt to drown herself, and the cause of her distress, the man who had brought her over from Japan, was named in the article. His real name was Strickland, and one of his business aliases was 'Churchill'. Even this could not shake the man's poise. Confronted by Miquel he explained that he had chosen his alias because it invariably brought a small, respectful flurry when he travelled by air and secured him his cherished objective, an invitation to visit the flight deck during the journey. As for the Japanese lady; well, he needed to learn Japanese and that was the best way to do it. Even then the saga was not over; there was the little matter of an expense-account entry entitled: 'Insurance on an aeroplane'. 'Churchill' had, it transpired, gone ahead with his Middle East project despite Miquel's refusal, and was now blithely billing Bell's for the privilege. He had to go, of course, but not without some regret. As a salesman he had given some leads to the Bell's export team, and in a short eighteen months he had helped establish markets for the firm which contributed to its long-term growth.

Having taken on export sales in 1968 Miquel began work on a strategic plan to expand and develop the export market. By 1973 a team of seven skilled overseas sales executives was in operation, covering all areas of the world. These seven were an elite team, highly paid, who always travelled first-class and stayed in five-star hotels. They were fully committed to the firm, and although they worked hard they were amply rewarded for their successes. Each man had his territory and was responsible for appointing agents, developing existing agents' activities and seeking new opportunities in the marketplace based on Bell's sales and marketing operation in the UK. An overseas sales co-ordinator at Head Office would prepare a brief for each market and respond to the debriefs which would be sent in by the overseas sales executives immediately after visiting a particular country. The overseas trips were on a six-week cycle, with between three and five days spent in each country, depending on the size and involvement. A typical visit would run as follows. First day: some twenty calls in retail outlets chosen at random to establish Bell's distribution in a major city, noting pricing and shelf position. Second day: meeting with the distributor or agent, using the information obtained the previous day. Third day: meeting customers arranged by the agent. Depending on the requirements in the marketplace, additional time could be spent with the agent. Then, at the end of each six-week tour, a week would be spent at Head Office with the co-ordinators, working on debriefs and briefs, culminating in a full day's meeting held on the Friday chaired by Miquel. Two weeks of 'trip leave' would then be taken by each executive before their next trip.

Mr Emori, President of Nihon Shurui Hunbai, Bell's agent in Japan, welcomes Miquel on a visit to Tokyo.

Miquel would read each overseas debrief, looking for missed opportunities or decisions taken outside company policy. Any offending sheet would be torn from the brief and kept for the bimonthly sales meeting, when the Chairman's comments would incorporate all the sheets. The team would learn from each individual comment made on all visits throughout the world. In the early days the list was quite extensive but latterly, as all sales executives came to ensure opportunities were taken and company policy followed, the lists dwindled. He himself visited overseas countries to hold meetings with Bell's agents during three months of every year. Three weeks were spent in Europe visiting on average the eight major countries, and there were also three two-week trips to the United States and one three-week trip to either Australasia, South America or the Far East. It was important that he should know each market fairly thoroughly to enable him to speak positively to the overseas executives.

On one unforgettable occasion during the 1970s a trip to visit Bell's Brazilian agents, Drury's SA, coincided with the famous Rio Carnival. Leaving Heathrow at 9.30 on the Sunday morning to catch the French Concorde in Paris, Miquel was amazed to be in Rio by 4.30 p.m. the same day. Drury's had insisted on meeting him and taking him straight to the main street where they had a box overlooking the parade, and by 6.30 he was watching a truly spectacular event. Each parade at Carnival can be up to half a mile long, and they represent township areas from all over the country. Points are awarded by a panel of judges for the different themes and standards of presentation, and one of the most important things they look for is the synchronisation of the four or five bands playing through the length of one parade. The tune for each parade is continuous and unique, so the band at the front has to be playing at the same place in the score as the band at the end. Each year the organisers set a new theme for Carnival, and it can take a township a full year to prepare its parade. It took almost 24 hours for the parades to pass, and his trip to Carnival remains one of Miquel's most spectacular memories from thirty years of overseas travel.

Business trips have provided him with many other entertaining experiences over the years, but his close encounter with the US security services remains a favourite. A regular visitor to the States, his trips were planned many weeks in advance and like many travelling executives, he was normally booked into the same hotel each time he visited a city. In Los Angeles this was the Century Plaza, where he was a familiar name and the Presidential Suite was always reserved for him wherever possible. He was aware, when he arrived there one Friday in 1980, that the Republican Party convention was to be held in the city in a few days' time, but he did not realise that Mondale, the leader of the Democrats, was holding a party rally there, and that both he and President Reagan with his entourage would be staying in the same hotel.

Returning from dinner on the Saturday evening the lifts stopped on the 19th floor and access to the suites, which were a floor above, was restricted to a small emergency stairway. At the top of the stairs Miquel was confronted by FBI guards who informed him that only White House officials could enter. Taken aback, Miquel insisted that he was booked into a room and after checking with the hotel manager the guards eventually let him through, advising him however that he would have to move out as Mondale had booked the entire floor for the Sunday and Monday and Reagan from Monday on. As Miquel wasn't leaving until the Tuesday morning he refused to move, and after much discussion with the FBI personnel and the hotel's management he was allowed to stay. Unfortunately there were a number of guards, none of whom appeared able or willing to pass the message on. Each time Miquel left or re-entered his suite he was stopped by a new, armed FBI agent, each highly suspicious of a foreigner apparently wandering around a secure area, and the hotel management had to be summoned to explain. It didn't help that Miquel was in training and left the hotel once a day in unprepossessing sports kit and running shoes, returning flushed and sweating later after a six-mile run round the streets of Los Angeles. The security guards made it clear that they saw him as some kind of spy.

On the Sunday morning he was awakened at 7.30 by the sitting-room doorbell, and opened the door to two dog-handlers with German Shepherd sniffer dogs, who insisted on entering and allowing the dogs to nose around the rooms. Then, the following evening, he came back from dinner to find Maureen Reagan's name on his door.

Fearful of entering he checked with the guards and learned that she wouldn't be arriving until the Tuesday. Relieved, he opened the door to find that details of the Republican electioneering activities that day had been slipped underneath, obviously left for the lady's attention when she arrived, and cases of Diet Coke had been placed in the bar in the sitting-room. This made all the business with the guards at the lift a little pointless, but Miquel forbore from pointing this out, convinced that it would only confuse them further. He did however consume a fair amount of the Diet Coke to wash away the dust of his training runs and soothe his throat, which was becoming rather sore from all the explanations. In the circumstances, he thought Ms Reagan would probably understand.

The success of the overseas sales operation was quite electrifying. Export sales rose from £4.4 million in 1973 to over £38 million in 1984, the majority of this growth being in the Bell's Scotch Whisky brand, despite the truism that brand-building is the most difficult way to develop sales. Bell's products were sold worldwide, with notable successes in Europe, Australia, Asia, South Africa and Latin America. Only in the US did a satisfactory market share elude them, thanks in part to legislation which forbade foreign exporters to deal directly with retailers or wholesalers in the American licensed trade. Bell's worked hard to establish the brand in the States via agents and its promotions did build the company a small market presence, but the company's long-term goal was to buy a US import company, giving it direct access to the market.

A major development in 1973 arose directly out of the company's increasing home sales. Between 1971 and 1973 home sales leapt from £21 million to over £37 million, with a further £4.4 million contribution from the developing export sales team. From 18 million bottles in 1970 Bell's was now selling almost double that number – by 1974 there would be 45 million bottles of Bell's sold worldwide. The company's requirement for Highland malt whisky now exceeded the capabilities of the existing three distilleries at Blair Athol, Inchgower and Dufftown, even though their output had tripled three years previously following the installation of new equipment. The board discussed the position and decided that Bell's should consider buying MacDonald Martin Co. Ltd, the owners of the Glenmorangie and

Glen Mhor malt whisky distilleries. It was agreed that Miquel should discuss the possibility with George Rattray, the chairman of the company, whom he knew quite well as they both sat on the Council of the Scotch Whisky Association. MacDonald Martin, although a public company, was controlled by the family trusts and Rattray was the family spokesperson. Miquel, accompanied by Bell's production director Gerry Gardner, went to meet Rattray, but he made it clear to Miquel that such a takeover was out of the question. This rebuttal disappointed Bell's, and rather than continue the search in the hope of finding another promising acquisition the board decided to ensure its Highland malt whisky supplies in another way. In 1974 a brand new distillery was built on a greenfield site at Dufftown, not far from the existing Dufftown-Glenlivet distillery whose high-quality water supply was vital to the production of a top-class malt whisky.

Pittyvaich-Glenlivet was a bold and innovative project. The new distillery's buildings, sited up on a hilltop, were designed and built around the equipment rather than vice-versa. It was a spacious, clean environment, ideal for efficient working, and produced Highland malt whisky of a quality one would expect from the respected Glenlivet name. With a capacity of over one million proof gallons per year, Pittyvaich-Glenlivet allowed the company to support its growing sales without the difficulties and upheavals of acquisition.

The building of Pittyvaich-Glenlivet solved Bell's malt whisky supply problems during the latter part of the 1970s, but although the firm was widening its interests through acquisition the core whisky business continued to grow. In 1976 a new bottling hall was built on a greenfield site in Dunfermline, and in 1980 the East Mains complex was extended and a new £2 million warehouse added. As late as 1983 it was to buy the Bladnoch distillery in Wigtown, which by then had been closed for three years. Bladnoch had several bonded storage warehouses and the intention behind the purchase was to eliminate the cost of storing the large quantities of grain whisky Bell's bought from William Grant's Girvan distillery each year. By transferring the casks when filled Bell's was able to achieve significant savings. Bladnoch was a bargain and provided ample storage space, but in addition Bell's decided to reopen the distilling operation and create work for twelve people at Wigtown. The company now had its own

Lowland malt distillery and after comprehensive renovations production was restarted in October 1983 at the rate of 700,000 gallons per year.

In 1967 Miquel had been appointed a member of the managing committee of the Malt Distillers' Association of Scotland. The Association, whose membership included virtually all the owners of the malt whisky distilleries in Scotland, was due to celebrate its centenary in 1974 and he was asked by the committee to chair meetings with a small group of members to develop ideas and organise events to celebrate the historic occasion. Sport as usual was to the fore and golf, football and curling competitions were introduced, to be played during 1974 between the various distilleries, culminating in a finals week in October.

There were three days of celebration from 8–10 October in Aviemore, and on the last night a special dinner was held in the banqueting hall of the Aviemore Centre, with Prince Philip as the guest of honour. The trophies for each sporting contest were presented to the winners during the evening and it proved a memorable occasion, uniting all Scotland's whisky distillers in a sense of togetherness. To mark the event Bell's asked each distiller to send a barrel of their best aged malt whisky to East Mains, and a special centenary malt blend was made from all the casks delivered. An appropriate label was designed and all members of the Association received a case of this precious bottled blend. To this day Miquel has kept two bottles of the blend which remain unopened.

1975 saw the 150th anniversary of Bell's founding and the birthday dinner at Glasgow's Albany Hotel was as much a celebration of the firm's present and future as of its past. More than five hundred employees from all the company's sites in Scotland were present, the first time such a gathering had been possible, and even the overseas sales team was recalled specially for the occasion. Two guests of honour, retired sisters who had spent their whole working lives with Bell's, recalled the company's modest centenary celebrations fifty years earlier. It was a happy evening, with cabaret by Ronnie Corbett and music from The Fourmost, a pop band who covered many of the popular chart hits of the day, and Raymond Miquel's speech reflected the upbeat mood of the company as he congratulated his staff on its

Cutting the cake at Bell's 150th anniversary celebrations.

outstanding success. The firm, he predicted, would continue to grow and prosper, and he looked forward with confidence to its 200th birthday dinner.

CHAPTER 3

Building the Brand

IN ONE OF THE MANY radio interviews he has done over the years, Miquel was asked about his management style. His answer was revealing. 'I studied all aspects of business, but I have to say that the marketing function, and particularly brand-building, have always attracted me far more than the day-to-day details of management. I don't think I would have enjoyed just managing a company.'

Even his most outspoken critics would concede that as a brand, Bell's under Miquel achieved spectacular success in both home and export markets. By 1980 the company had a home market share of almost 25%, when Bell's was the most recognised blend of Scotch, miles ahead of its nearest competitor. Sales rose year on year, often in the face of the downward market trend, and in 1984, the last full year before the Guinness takeover bid, pre-tax profits were at an all-time high of £35.2 million. Central to this success, and indeed to Miquel's whole approach to business, was a management strategy that put brand image at the heart of company policy and looked to the details to get an edge on the competition.

Bell's had never gone in for glitzy advertising and Miquel had no intention of sending the firm down that road. They didn't have that kind of money, and besides, he couldn't see the point of doing things the same way the competition did. The thing that had made the most impression on him was when, at college, they were asked to think about successful brand images. 'We were talking about everyday brand names, like the Bisto Kids, for instance, or Coca-Cola and Mars, and I started wondering about the guys who first thought them up, and how they must have stood out at the time. The whole thing was about being different from all your competitors.' Miquel encouraged his people to think creatively: 'Look at what the others are doing,' he told them, 'and if someone else is doing it, we don't.' So Bell's press and poster adverts remained plain and inexpensive: display advertising featured simple illustrations, cartoons and line drawings for the most part, and always the 'Afore Ye Go . . ! ' which was and is to Bell's what 'St Michael' is to Marks and Spencer. Television commercials were not an option as there was an agreement amongst all the members of the Scotch Whisky Association that they would not use this medium for advertising, an agreement that was rescinded in the 1990s. This was an advantage to Bell's as in the 1960s it would not have been able to afford the expense of running a good campaign, unlike some of its competitors.

Miquel regarded advertising first and foremost as a way of putting the brand consistently before the public, and to this end he was able to use small, inexpensive opportunities to good effect. One very successful policy was that of buying the 'corner spaces' – the small boxes at the top of a newspaper's front page, one on either side of the masthead. From 1965 to 1975 Bell's booked all available doubles of these spaces, mainly on Saturdays, for weeks ahead in papers like the *Mirror, Telegraph, Guardian, Mail, Times, Scotsman* and *Herald*, ensuring that 'Bell's Scotch Whisky' would appear prominently, flanking the paper's name and immediately visible to anyone glancing at the front page. Since the many newspaper shops used tiered wire display racks outside their doors, the result was a display of daily papers on which passers-by saw 'Bell's Scotch Whisky' repeated over and over again down the length of the rack. Another good strategy in the 1970s was to advertise on the new TV listings pages which papers had started producing for Easter, Christmas and Bank Holidays. The centre spread would be given over to radio and television programmes and Bell's negotiated for a new advertising position, a strip along the top and bottom of such pages, again bearing the simple message 'Bell's Scotch Whisky'. These were the rare times when Bell's advertised inside a newspaper or magazine – usually the rule was front or back page solus position only. This creative approach to advertising space was Bell's hallmark. Before billboards on football grounds were established Bell's negotiated with Willie Waddell, the then manager of Glasgow Rangers, to put large boards with the words 'Bell's Scotch Whisky' along their length either side of the centre line at Rangers' Ibrox ground. Although the idea was new, Waddell saw it as additional income for the club. Celtic also agreed to accept the boards and as these teams' matches were frequently shown on the Saturday evening

TV sports report it was great exposure for Bell's. The company soon negotiated for similar boards on the pitches for all home international games and as it was first in the field, Bell's was able to contract for the special positions for years ahead.

A weekly advertising meeting chaired by Miquel was held every Friday when he was not overseas, and went on late into the evening. These meetings were used to develop all the company's creative ideas, and meant that the effectiveness of all the firm's advertising was kept constantly under review.

One instance where Bell's did spend serious money on advertising was the Sunday supplements. In 1969 Sunday papers had not reached their current mammoth proportions but they were still prestigious advertising space, particularly the tabloid colour supplement which many had adopted. Rivals like Teachers made frequent use of them but Bell's had never done so, largely because of the enormous cost – £4300 for the back page. There was at that time a growing fashion for mixed drinks, although mixing Scotch was still widely held as sacrilege and the only acceptable additions to a glass of whisky were ice and water. Drinks adverts tended to focus on how you served the product, those for whisky urging drinkers to 'Drink it with ice or water' or other conservative suggestions. When in that year Miquel decided to advertise in the supplements Bell's advert read: 'Drink it with water, lemonade, ginger ale or soda. Bell's – the broad-minded Scotch.' This, he explains with a smile, provoked consternation among his colleagues on the Council of the Scotch Whisky Association, to which he had only just been appointed, as it seemed to denigrate the image of Scotch whisky. Bell's deliberately used couples in this particular advertisement, to reflect the fact that ladies were now drinking Scotch with mixers.

One reason for Bell's conspicuous success at brand-building was its attention to detail across the board, which formed an integral part of the company culture. The relatively modest advertising was effective because it was part of a highly co-ordinated overall brand image reinforced by PR and promotion. The point-of-sale material provided by the on-trade was a good example of this; like its competitors, Bell's ensured ashtrays, beermats, water-jugs, bar towels and the like were available to licensees, each printed with the Bell's Scotch Whisky name in the company colours of red, white and black. This was nothing new, but few companies at the time went to the lengths Bell's did to keep the range in line with the brand image. Great emphasis was laid on high print quality and colour-matching of batches, allowing new items to fit seamlessly into the range so the customer always saw the same message, reinforcing his or her awareness of the brand. Miquel recalls that after the Guinness takeover he produced a presentation for Ernest Saunders, with illustrations of the entire Bell's point-of-sale and promotional range. The Guinness chairman expressed admiration for Bell's approach and asked Miquel to conducted a review of Guinness's own point-of-sale. After a visit to the Guinness marketing department at Park Royal in London he reported poor standardisation, and a remarkable lack of coherence in that company's promotional materials. Bell's message may have been simple, but that was no bad thing, and it definitely gave the brand a recognition factor head and shoulders above most of its competitors.

Another important mainstay of the Bell's image was the bottle label. There were a number of variations of this, depending on bottle size, but the basic Bell's label had endured few changes since its inception in the 1920s and Miquel resisted all temptation to tamper with it more than was necessary. In his view it embodied the brand and was, therefore, sacrosanct. Competitors such as McKinley's brought in bright modern labels, but Bell's policy was to stay with the same design, believing that any changes would adversely affect the image of tradition and quality the company was striving to convey to its customers. Asked about the current Bell's label – the latest of several the brand has worn since the takeover – he expresses only qualified admiration. 'It's a nice-looking label, but to me it doesn't project the traditional image of Bell's Scotch Whisky.'

Advertising and brand image would always be central to the firm's marketing and PR strategy, but new ideas, particularly ones which brought social or community benefits as well as good publicity, were eagerly discussed and many were seized on by competitors to become common industry practice. Miquel's way of organising and running the company, however, would always remain controversial, attracting admirers and critics in equal measure, and few were bold enough to experiment with the formula for themselves.

One of Miquel's more radical strategies was his sales policy. This, in its simplest form, read: 'No discounting – no deals'. Bell's had ambitious plans for the home market; the brand was popular in Scotland when Miquel took over, but there was an enormous amount to be done in the rest of the UK, and no brewery group was willing to discuss letting that type of premium brand in through the front door of their tied premises, as many small distillers were finding to their cost. For a large company or conglomerate the solution would be an expensive launch, massive discounting in the short term with advertising and promotional support, and big incentives for the reps. Giveaways – offering cheap or free cases of the brand on the back of a more established name – was another legitimate strategy. Bell's had neither the funds nor the will to force itself into the game this way and Miquel had no intention of compromising Bell's premium image by selling it cheaply, or tying it to any other brand name. Instead, the onus was placed on the salespeople to establish personal contact with individual licensees and publicans in tenanted houses who could not buy Bell's from their local brewery, and convince them to order it from a local wholesaler if the brewery refused to supply it. As demand for Bell's grew the brewers at central head office saw Scotch whisky sales declining and they were forced to stock Bell's to supply to their tenants. The old guard thought this policy sound enough, but when Miquel laid down the conditions under which salespeople would be employed, and the rules governing their dealings with customers, there were questions. There would be no bonuses or incentives; Bell's reps were to be salaried, and while they had targets to meet they received no financial incentives for volume sold. Nor were they permitted to do price deals with the customer. Bell's would quote one price for all its customers, so that all had the same opportunity to earn a wholesale discount through high volume sales. As far as Miquel is aware nobody else in the industry did things this way at the time, and certain individuals were quick to predict disaster as a result. Where would the reps' motivation come from? How would they attract good experienced salesmen if no bonuses were on offer? And even if they did manage to get a sales team together, how would they persuade buyers to take a premium brand at a premium price unless they could sweeten the initial deal with a discount? Miquel was adamant, and dissenters were left in no doubt as to what was expected of them. 'It's the company that must dictate how you operate. It's not what you want, it's what the company requires that matters.'

One great advantage of Bell's sales policy was that it offended nobody. Since customers could not arrange special deals, they soon realised that no one was receiving preferential treatment and dealings with them became more efficient and businesslike than the traditional haggling game. Under Miquel Bell's took this policy further, avoiding all the usual sort of customer hospitality. The sales director never took his major clients to sporting fixtures or the opera, because Miquel had no time for the politics that would inevitably follow. 'Whoever we took, someone else would have complained because we hadn't asked them, so we didn't participate. We concentrated on raising the profile of the brand across the board.' Far from alienating retailers, the new arrangements actually proved attractive in the long term, because new potential buyers saw their business as being of equal value to Bell's as that of more established customers, and knew they would be able to sell their new brand at a regular price because their margins would be roughly the same as the other retailers. Secondly, it removed the short-termism inherent in the sales rep's job. A salesman's authority to barter with his customer can result in creative and profitable deals, but it also leads inevitably to secrecy, favouritism, and mutual back-scratching. Heavy discounting may increase volume, but also increases the potential for long-term damage to the brand image.

The licensed trade has altered greatly in recent years. Legislation intended to promote competition has led large brewery companies to divest themselves of many of their public houses, and publicans are no longer forced to sell only the brewery's brands of spirits as they were in the sixties when the tie between producers and retailers was very strong. For some publicans, however, some things never change: it is still a demanding business to be in, with long and unsocial hours, poor pay, and for those who live over the shop, an uncertain future as retirement looms. These and other factors have made it a clannish and well-organized trade, complete with specialist publications and active trade associations which promote and defend the interests of their members. Under Miquel, Bell's was the first whisky firm to recognise the potential offered by the licensed trade as a whole, and to build a comprehensive policy of trade relations into its business. The aim was to promote the company and its product at a grass-roots level by winning the support of the licensees and retailers, and to reinforce this through liaison with the trade organisations which supported them. Friendly relations were established with the Licensed Victuallers' National Homes, the main trade charity at the time, and throughout Miquel's tenure the firm was to be generous in its support of the various trades associations' causes. Miquel himself served terms first as Chairman of the Scottish Licensed Trade Association in 1971, and then in 1976 as President of the Licensed Victuallers' National Homes Association, when he helped raise an unprecedented £360,000 for the charity during his year of office, including a record £105,000 raised by Bell's itself for the President's List. Later, in 1980 he took on the presidency of the Licensed Victuallers' School in Slough and a busy President's Year followed, in which £124,000 was raised for LV School funds. These were not straightforward donations but were raised through special events throughout the year, often with the enthusiastic support of Bell's workforce. Pub collections were common, using empty Bell's gallon bottles, but high-profile sporting events were also arranged in which Miquel, as chairman, was a willing participant.

In September 1976, during Miquel's year as president of the LVNH, Bell's organised an evening athletics meeting in Gateshead for which Brendan Foster set up the arrangements. A number of British stars competed at the 'Bell's Whisky Games', including Geoff Capes, Ainslie Bennett, Alan Pascoe, David Jenkins and Brendan Foster himself, and they were joined by athletes from other countries, notably the US Olympic runner and former world record holder Jim Bolding. The evening featured a 2000-metre steeplechase special event in which Miquel had to complete the course – which included five water jumps and fifteen hurdles – in under 8 minutes 40 seconds. For every second under that time each sponsor agreed to pay £1 to the charity. Arriving at the ground with his sports bag Miquel went straight to the changing room, where the night's famous names were already preparing for their events. He recalls with a smile the puzzled glances he attracted as he entered; it was obvious the other athletes thought this unknown forty-four-year-old was in the wrong place. A wandering member of the audience? The groundsman, perhaps? Their

In action at Gateshead . . . made it by 8 seconds.

confusion only increased when the new arrival calmly opened his bag, took out his running kit and began to change. 'I did have an athlete's body,' he explains, 'just not the young man's face to go with it!'

In addition to the prize money, Bell's had advised competitors, the winner of each event would receive a gallon bottle of Bell's Scotch Whisky. For Miquel's own race Gateshead Harriers had supplied four runners from their steeplechase team to pace him and help him achieve his target. It was a very wet evening and the track was not well lit, but on his third lap Miquel was surprised to realise that the Harriers appeared to be leaving him behind. He stepped up his pace and managed to keep up with one of them, and was later to learn that Bell's Marketing Services director had offered the gallon bottle to the so-called 'helpers', hence their anxiety to reach the finishing line! On the final lap Miquel clipped one of the hurdles, fell but rolled over and quickly regained his feet, pressing on towards the finishing line. He assumed the target was lost, but in fact he finished in an incredible 8 minutes 32 seconds, raising £8 per sponsor and a total of more than £7000 for charity. There was a celebration dinner dance that night for all participants and the trade members, but much of Miquel's evening was spent in the Casualty department of the local hospital, where x-rays revealed that he had broken his arm in five places in the fall. He returned to the ball at midnight complete with plaster cast, and the incident attracted wide coverage the following day in the local and trade press.

In the same year Miquel had played six-times world snooker champion Ray Reardon at four separate venues around the UK. The events generated around £6000 for the LVNH, and was the start of a friendly rivalry between the two men. These events were repeated in 1980, during Miquel's term as president of the LV School, and raised a similar amount for the cause.

During his presidency of the LV School he had another memorable celebrity challenge. In May 1980 he raced against Alan Pascoe in front of a thousand spectators at the LV School sports day, taking on the new European Olympic hurdles champion in a 2400-metre handicap in which he would run six laps to Pascoe's seven. Much to Miquel's surprise he realised that he was able to match the champion's pace, and by lap five Pascoe was a scant 100 metres ahead. Greatly encouraged by this, and aware of the chance of an excellent publicity photo for the LV School cause, Miquel put on a burst of speed in his final lap and caught Pascoe right on the line – the latter, of course, still having an extra lap to run. The event raised £9500 for the LVNH School. It also gave Miquel a short-lived taste of sports celebrity, as all the young autograph-hunters who had been besieging Pascoe now clamoured for the signature of the middle-aged man who had held him to a draw. There was no danger of a swollen ego, however; the young 'fans' were quick to point out that they didn't want the signature themselves but for their mums!

Bell's support for the LVA charities helped win the company the respect and gratitude of the licensed trade. Its interest in providing for old and vulnerable ex-licensees was particularly commended, and was seen inside and outside the firm as a logical extension of the old ties with the Gannochy Estate. The first of the LVNH's estates in Scotland would be built opposite the Blair Athol distillery at Pitlochry in 1980, on land donated by the company, and was named the Arthur Bell Estate in honour of the gift and the associated Deed of Covenant

A close finish with Alan Pascoe.

After the race — a clamour for autographs.

The opening of the Arthur Bell estate on the Isle of Man.

which took care of the upkeep. In 1982 another estate was financed by Bell's, this time on the Isle of Man.

The company's involvement brought it quantities of favourable publicity, particularly in the Trade press, and helped develop a genuine affection for the brand amongst the publicans, who appreciated the personal effort put into the fundraising by Bell's staff and chairman. This was apparent after his successful year as chairman of the LVNH, when the licensed trade elected Miquel its wholesaler Personality of the Year in 1977 and invited him to the annual gala lunch to receive his award. The invitation was made a little tentatively, however, as the sponsors for the event were J & B, and the prize consisted of six bottles of J & B Rare Old Scotch Whisky. Would Mr Miquel wish to accept them?

Nominations and votes for these awards had come from the individual licensees themselves, so they did represent the feeling of the grass-roots of the trade, with whom Miquel had always tried to maintain cordial relations. He felt genuinely pleased to be offered the award and wanted very much to attend the ceremony, but unfortunately the lunch fell in the middle of one of his trips to the

United States. A compromise was eventually reached, and so at around five-thirty in the morning Miquel found himself sitting up in bed in the Beverley Hills Hotel in Los Angeles, waiting for a phone call that would link him live with the presentation lunch at a top London hotel. When the receptionist eventually rang up to tell him his call had come through, she asked him what was going on. The line had been open for several minutes and she had heard the babble of happy voices and several loud choruses of 'Land of Hope and Glory' from the assembled audience. 'I'm from the UK myself,' she explained, 'and I'm homesick. I've been sitting here listening and having a little weep.' At this point Miquel's cue arrived and he made a gracious acceptance speech to the assembled licensees, mainly ladies. A satellite video link might perhaps have had more impact, but the telephone did allow him the unique experience of giving a formal address to a roomful of women from his bed, wearing only a hotel sheet.

At an individual level, sales executives were carefully selected for their quality and trained to develop a rapport with the customer. Salaries were high, so suitable candidates could be recruited and retained which meant that Bell's customers came to know and trust their rep. This friendly relationship was backed up by a growing budget to underwrite Bell's commitment to its customers. Since the firm did not take the favoured few on jamborees it could concentrate instead on reaching the many, and this was done mainly by promotional tasting evenings for groups of licensees, complete with film show and publicity and the cracking of a Bell's gallon collecting bottle, which usually yielded around £300 for charity. Press calls were given a high priority in the salespeople's schedule; in fact, they were set targets for news coverage of these events, and a six-monthly awards scheme was established to reward those reps whose face had appeared most times in the press during that period. The average was around 50, and as Bell's employed 50 salespersons the coverage would equate to around 2500 pictures in a six-month period appearing in local press throughout the country. One particularly successful salesman, John Rutherford, once managed 133 different captioned press photographs over a six-month period, and easily carried off the framed original caricature which went to the winner of the gold award. The constant

Alan Whicker and Ray Reardon toast the completion
of 'Whicker in Bell's World'.

trickle of positive coverage generated by this policy was invaluable in raising the profile of the brand at a local level.

As part of the promotional strategy Miquel had a publicity film made, and for some years tasting evenings incorporated a showing of 'A Proud Heritage'. The firm's rapid expansion eventually dated the film and in 1981 it was replaced by a more ambitious project. Journalist and TV presenter Alan Whicker, of ITV's 'Whicker's World', brought his famous documentary format to Bell's operations and produced a 30-minute company film, 'Whicker in Bell's World'. This was a real coup because Whicker, whose distinctive broadcasting style and quirky outlook were extremely popular with audiences, was at first reluctant even to consider the project when approached by Miquel and Tony Derry, who sought him out at his home in Jersey during a business trip. He was busy with broadcasting and writing commitments, he explained, and had no time or energy to commit to commercial promotions. However, the men's description of Bell's unique business philosophy, particularly its charitable and community activities, roused his interest and he eventually agreed to meet Miquel and Derry in London for an escorted trip to Perth. The result was 'Whicker in Bell's World', directed and produced by Whicker's own team, which neatly captured the unique nature of the company and its successful fusion of the traditional and the modern.

As the firm's facilities grew and improved, information and visitor hospitality had been incorporated into the plan. When the hospitality centre opened at Cherrybank in 1979, with its outstanding facilities and landscaped gardens, parties of customers from the licensed trade began to arrive regularly for tours, tastings, entertainment and a chance to meet the Bell's team. 'Whicker in Bell's World' fitted neatly into the experience and over the years many thousands of visitors must have enjoyed Alan Whicker's very personal look at the Bell's operation.

Bell's image as a successful Scottish independent was promoted enthusiastically by the company, since it was a part of the quality image which enabled premium branding and a matching price. The phrase 'a quality Scottish company' was frequently used by Miquel, particularly during the 1982 takeover battle for Gleneagles Hotels. The company's attitude to visitors was typical of this. 'Afore Ye Go . . ! ' remained the firm's motto, recalling the duty of hospitality owed by a Highland host to his guest, and this was particularly true once the Cherrybank facilities opened and visiting parties could be entertained in-house. Unlike all other major Scotch whisky companies Bell's steadfastly refused to open a London office. All visitors, both home and overseas, discussed business and were entertained in the Perth office in Scotland by the company's management and staff. There were accusations of overwork and exploitation from observers who saw only the long hours; paradoxically, visitors would often comment on the pleasant, informal atmosphere in Bell's offices and factories and the approachability of top management, by whom the 'open door' policy was taken very seriously. Visitors were encouraged, welcomed, fed, entertained and sent away content, and the costs incurred cheerfully as a vital part of building the brand.

One innovation which was copied was the launch of the 'Greenjackets'. Bell's salesmen were required to attend many trade events, banquets, company hospitality evenings and the like in the course of their duties, where they and their rivals from other firms would meet customers and potential customers in a social setting. Such events were generally regarded as a perk, not working time, but Miquel was determined this should not be the case with his own people. 'I've never had much time for the lunching and golfing approach to business. When you attend an event like this then you are at work, and you should behave as though you are. That means you look after your customers.' At most licensed trade functions he attended he sat at the top table and soon realised that far from looking after buyers and licensees, the majority of sales staff present from other companies were chatting with their supposed rivals or hovering around the hospitality girls. There and then he decided to ensure that his own staff took advantage of the laxity of the competition. A smart green dinner jacket was designed, and each sales executive was required to wear one at all official functions from then on, making Bell's staff immediately identifiable to customers and to their own management. The step could have caused resentment, but in actual fact it was an excellent move which worked in two ways. The uniforms allowed easy identification and encouraged potential customers to approach staff, while projecting a smart corporate image which reflected well on Bell's. Staff who behaved unprofessionally on duty could be quickly spotted and pulled up, and Miquel recalls salesmen sent home from conventions for spending their time chatting to hospitality girls or otherwise misbehaving in uniform. There were often around a thousand people at such conventions, but the Greenjackets could be seen with their customers throughout, and attended an evening briefing beforehand and then a debrief at midnight, when the event was over. Those who wore the jacket gained a reputation as sober, businesslike and attentive to their customers, and the Greenjackets came to be regarded as an elite, which made the green jacket itself a huge incentive amongst salespeople anxious to join the ranks of the favoured. 'Our sales people were known as the gentlemen of the trade,' recalls Raymond Miquel, 'and I was proud of that.' Needless to say the competition followed suit, and before long there was a positive kaleidoscope of jackets at any Trade event, including the blue of White & Mackay and the grey of McKinley's.

Far from resenting this, however, Miquel was quite happy, since it tended to highlight their inadequacies and make it even more obvious which company's representatives were doing their job and which were not. Bell's green jackets were the first, and considering that their salaried occupants competed for the privilege without any other incentive than the pride of wearing them, they could truly be seen as unique.

One of the salespeople's advantages in those early days was the gallon bottle of Scotch, first mass-produced by Bell's after Miquel spotted a one-off being used for promotional purposes and brought it back to head office. The idea was that they could be used in pubs for collecting money, but they proved so popular on optics that the company found itself making far more than had originally been planned. The size was almost scuppered before it took off; in 1971 a meeting of the Council of the Scotch Whisky Association was reluctant to include the gallon on a list of approved bottle sizes compiled for forthcoming European legislation. None of the other producers used gallons, and there was little support for them amongst their representatives at the meeting. Miquel had been appointed to the Association in 1968, joining other managing directors of large Scotch whisky companies, eight from the independents and eight from the giant Distillers' Corporation Ltd, with DCL's chairman also chairing the Council at that time. Miquel's was the only voice raised in support for the gallon size, but he was voted down by others at the meeting and the giant bottles did not appear on the list of recommendations. This was to be typical of his relations with the Scotch Whisky Association. Ignoring the implied criticism Bell's continued to produce gallons, and it is interesting to note that by the end of the decade the gallon featured prominently on the Association's list of approved sizes, due largely to the gallon's popularity on optics in the pubs. The gallon bottles had proved one of Bell's – and later the whisky industry's – most useful marketing tools.

At the opening of Deanston Distillery in 1964 Miquel met his lecturer in marketing from his early days in college. He told him that although his many ideas for trade sales (i.e. within the licensed trade) were working well, he lacked a medium for getting to the consumers and the retail sector as Bell's was a little-known product in England.

Nothing further was said at the time, but some two years later, quite out of the blue, the same man called Miquel at home at eleven one evening to say that he had come across just the promotion he was looking for. It seemed that Westclox presented a trophy to a selected football manager once a year but had decided the scheme had little publicity value. Would Bell's like to take on the promotion? Initially the idea made little impression on Miquel, but after spending one hour on the telephone discussing proposals for the scheme's development, such as planning a 'Manager of the Month' presentation for each football division leading up to annual divisional awards and an overall Manager of the Year, he recognised the potential and decided to take it further. The public relations executive who helped develop the scheme with Miquel was John Watt, who was responsible for implementing the arrangements as the ideas flowed through. He did this with a great deal of success as he had a very strong rapport with the media and the Football Association.

The mechanics of the awards scheme were soon in place and the Bell's Scotch Whisky Football Managers Awards were launched in the 1968/69 football season. Selections were made by a panel of 25 top sports writers which brought the media onside, and presentations to the monthly winners were made at home matches, taking advantage of the assembled photographers and TV crews and ensuring they were covered by most newspapers' sports pages. A bonus for Bell's was that the majority of the football league clubs were soon carrying a piece about the awards in their match programmes as they speculated about the possibility of their manager receiving an award. A handsome silver cup three inches taller than the European Cup was designed by Miquel's creative team and was presented to the Manager of the Year, along with a cheque for £5000, at the annual charity shield match between the winners of the League and the FA Cup. The cup itself was insured for £70,000. There was also an annual awards lunch, covered by ITV's World of Sport, to which all 91 Football League managers were invited, and it was always a sell-out. Over the years the speakers included Eric Morecambe, Bill Shankly, Ian St John, Bob Paisley, the sports writer Hugh McIlvanney and many other famous names from the world of football.

The Bell's Football Managers Awards caught the imagination of the

Don Revie receiving the first Bell's Scotch Whisky Football Manager of the Year Award.

English football world and took the Bell's name straight to the public, just as Miquel had hoped. It also, understandably, gave the brand a special place in the affections of the football managers themselves. Ron Atkinson, then manager of Manchester United, was interviewed on BBC radio on the morning of the 1983 Milk Cup and recalled a visit to Old Trafford by rival manager Bob Paisley. Atkinson invited the Liverpool boss into his office and asked what he would have to drink. 'Could I have a small Bell's?' enquired Paisley. 'Sorry, Bob,' replied Atkinson, 'I haven't any in – you've got it all.' Spoken in jest, but Bob Paisley's managerial awards from Bell's at that time numbered 22 in total.

Unfortunately the scheme was not as successful in Scotland as it was in England. The original strategy had included awards for the two Scottish divisions as well, but the Scottish FA insisted on a meeting with Bell's and demanded £25,000 per year if Bell's, which had already

Alex Ferguson, then manager of Aberdeen, with his special award at the Bell's Football Manager of the Year Award Luncheon. On the right is Dundee United manager, Jim McLean.

made two monthly presentations in Scotland, wanted to continue with the awards. This was totally unacceptable; the awards themselves amounted to several thousands of pounds, and a disappointed Miquel decided to abandon the Scottish part of the scheme. However, it was the English market that Bell's really wanted to penetrate and the English awards scheme would remain an important feature in Bell's marketing. In the 1983–84 season it was extended into Spain when Bell's Spanish agent set up a scheme with the Spanish media, and Terry Venables' successful spell at Barcelona brought him several gallon bottles and Bell's more coverage both in Spain and at home in Britain. 'There was no other scheme to recognise sporting heroes when we first began,' Miquel recalls, 'but soon all the high-profile sports – cricket, golf, horse racing and so on – had their own monthly awards.' Of all the promotions Bell's did this was the one which was best remembered, and which perhaps best illustrates the firm's ability to turn a simple idea into successful public relations.

In the days of ITV's World of Sport programme on Saturday afternoons the Bell's Manager of the Year luncheon presentations received excellent live coverage. Organising the annual event with World of Sport executives meant that John Bromley, who was head of the department, and Raymond Miquel became good friends. When John heard of Bell's team sporting prowess he challenged the firm to twelve-a-side sporting weekend and this soon became an annual fixture. The World of Sport team included Billy Wright, Ian St John, Mick McManus, Raleigh Gilbert, Derek Thompson and John Bromley himself; Miquel led the Bell's team. The event included tennis, squash, snooker and golf competitions. Bell's invariably ended up winning the event; however the weekend at Gleneagles always afforded great enjoyment and established a strong relationship between the programme heads, ensuring Bell's would get the TV coverage which would help to promote its product.

The list of Bell's innovative promotions is endless, but several others

The World of Sport team with the Bell's team.

deserve a particular mention for their originality. When Bell's took its whisky to the Ideal Home Exhibition in 1969 it raised a few eyebrows, since no one had ever considered the show a good platform for food or drink, but the company had long understood the concept of 'lifestyle' and knew that it was affecting customers' purchasing decisions in the drinks market just as in any other. Its presence at the Exhibition was intended to take the Bell's brand to a large, captive English audience and gain some valuable brand exposure in the South of England, and at the same time associate it in the public's mind with quality living. The aim was for maximum impact, and the media were quick to latch on to the story. The company's 'Bell's Bellringer' was the late ex-RSM Ronald Brittain, a huge and imposing man famed for possessing the loudest voice of command in the British Army during his Service years. Now, resplendent in his braided uniform, he attended Bell's functions to proclaim the virtues of the product and at the Ideal Home Exhibition he marched eight promotions girls in tartan mini-kilts to the stand each morning. There were hourly competitions throughout the day with bottles of Bell's as a prize, as

A draw for the raffle competition at the Ideal Homes Exhibition with Bell's Toastmaster, RSM Ronald Brittain at the back.

well as repeated screenings of the company film, and the entire event proved very successful in publicity terms.

So too did the Bell's Thames sailing barge whose distinctive shape and red sails with 'Bell's Scotch Whisky' prominently displayed became a familiar sight at regattas and other events all around the South Coast during the summer months. It was introduced in the late sixties and each year it would be moored at Tower Pier for two weeks to enable Bell's to play host to civic officials, parties from the licensed trade, and Members of both Houses of Parliament. In 1978 Bell's purchased *Hydrogen*, one of the last remaining Thames sailing barges, and Sir Alex Rose, the first round-the-world yachtsman, officially launched the restored and refitted barge in 1980. It became part of the summer scene on the South coast and a great publicity tool for Bell's.

A foiled, bell-shaped swing ticket on a thread was introduced as part of the packaging of the Bell's bottle during the 1960s. The tickets, which hung around the neck of the bottle, became popular with some

Bill Walker, MP for Perth and East Perthshire, (left) and the Earl of Mansfield, Minister of State, Scottish Office, take the wheel of the Bell's Scotch Whisky Sailing Barge Hydrogen *at Tower Pier.*

bartenders who displayed them in decorative designs at the back of their bars. This gave Miquel the idea that if he introduced a series of famous bells, one on each ticket, it would create more interest. These quickly became popular amongst the public, and 48 different bells of worldwide interest were used on the tickets.

Frustrated collectors unable to find a particular ticket began to write to the company asking for swaps, and a member of staff at the firm's publicity agents was given the job of replying to correspondence and co-ordinating a Bell's swap-shop. The collectors wrote keen, cheerful letters to this individual who replied in kind, and interest was such that it was decided to launch an official 'Bell's Collectors' Club' to capitalise on all this goodwill and interest in the brand. A collectors' scrapbook was produced, with slots for all 48 tickets to fit in and further background material. Collectors who completed the set could send in their finished book and receive a package of promotional goodies, including a bell-shaped gold key chain and the company history, *Pride of Perth*. Before long there were 25,000 registered collectors, far more than the agency could deal with, and a department had eventually to be set up at Cherrybank to deal with the club's administration.

The personal emphasis remained, however, and when Miquel realised that a sizeable number of collectors were actually sending Christmas cards to their Club contact at Bell's, he felt the company should respond. A Collectors' Club Christmas card was produced, and at the time of the takeover by Guinness Bell's was sending out over 50,000 cards a year to registered collectors. Bell's bottles no longer bear the swing ticket – they were discontinued soon after the takeover – but the Collector's Club promotion is still remembered as an excellent example of its kind, particularly since it raised awareness in the company and its product in groups not normally associated with the Scotch whisky market. Miquel recalls one particular letter from a teacher whose class had completed the collection as a special project, thanking the company for the interesting material it had provided and explaining that after so much searching and collecting, the children were disappointed to learn that the exercise was complete. Did Bell's not, she asked a little plaintively, have some other interesting promotion they could begin instead?

Thelma Seear, through her PR company, had dealt with several of Bell's promotional activities. She organised the barge tours, the Ideal Home Exhibition stand and all Bell's financial press conferences. She lived in London and through her connections in the press she was able to organise with the then Secretary of the House of Commons Press Gallery, Gordon Campbell, an annual Burns Night whisky tasting in the Press Gallery bar. This was an opportunity for Miquel to meet Cabinet Ministers and Members of Parliament, and to project Bell's successful progress. At an appropriate moment he would address the gathering and present the Chairman of the Press Gallery with a Bell's decanter.

In image terms Bell's was riding high. One of Miquel's last and proudest publicity coups came in 1982 when the firm was offered the opportunity to sponsor the Ryder Cup, the premier three-day golfing challenge that sees Britain and Europe's top golfing professionals pitted against the US team. Golf and Scotland are synonymous, of course, even though the Americans had long since established

Miquel with Michael Foot at the Burns Night Tasting of Bell's Scotch Whisky for Members of the Parliamentary Press Gallery in 1977.

themselves as the almost inevitable winners of the Ryder Cup, and as Bell's inched closer to acquiring a company which would give it entry to the US liquor market there was an obvious advantage in sponsoring an event which would give the company high-profile coverage on both sides of the Atlantic.

The tournament is held every other year, in Europe and the United States alternately, and generates live TV coverage for many of the matches and extensive recorded highlights throughout, but although it offers prime exposure to sponsors it is an expensive affair. In 1982 the Cup's previous sponsors had decided not to renew their support and the tournament appeared under threat, but when Bell's stepped in to underwrite the next two Cups it was entirely a business decision, not a matter of sentiment. Bell's was already involved with the PGA, the sport's governing body, supporting PGA cup matches at the Scottish courses of Muirfield and Turnberry and running a popular junior golf tournament as part of its sporting and community commitments. The Ryder Cup deal committed Bell's to sponsorship of the next two Ryder tournaments, which would both be billed as the Bell's Ryder Cup. This cost the company £300,000, but Miquel was convinced the prestige and high profile of the event made it a smart promotional choice. The substantial sponsorship money enabled the European team to be decked out in standard uniforms, both for the golf and daily wear. Special golf bags with the players' names on were produced for the occasion and the team, with their wives, flew by Concorde to the USA in 1983. The new image did a great deal to boost the morale of the team as they no longer looked like the poor relations when compared to their USA opponents. The 1983 event in Florida had been a thrilling affair, with the European team beaten by the narrowest of margins, but now the company's PR people were working towards the 1985 Cup, due to take place in September 1985 at the Belfry course not far from Birmingham.

The tournament received considerable media coverage and the European team's victory was headline news. Miquel made the presentation speech live on TV from the Belfry in front of thousands of spectators who had gathered to witness the event. Previously, in August 1984, Tony Jacklin (the European Ryder team captain) had taken a day out from a stay at Gleneagles to visit Cherrybank for

With Ryder Cup Captains, Lee Trevino and Tony Jacklin, at the Belfry in 1985.

With the victorious European Ryder Cup team of 1985.

lunch, and struck the inaugural putt on the gardens' pitch-and-putt course. It seemed like a good omen.

Bell's quality image was vigorously defended. The brand was expensive in retail outlets and price-cutting was heavily discouraged – the absence of wholesale discounting was an important factor in this. Miquel also appreciated the importance of retail merchandising; in addition to their other duties Bell's salesmen made twenty retail calls a day to monitor their brand against the competition. The company was not prepared to spend its promotional money on cutting prices but it was happy to pay for an eye-level position and product facings. Customers were encouraged to think of Bell's as *the* quality blended Scotch, which was reflected in the high retail price, and this approach to retail sales paid off in the pubs where all blends were priced the same, so customers asked by name for the blend they perceived as good quality and value for money.

In 1970 Bell's home whisky sales totalled £18.8 million. By 1976 this had risen to £96.2 million, slightly more than a fivefold increase, and over the same period profits went from £1.5 million to £11.5 million, and this in an industry popularly accepted to be at best stagnant and at worst in decline. By 1980 Bell's was the leading blended Scotch whisky in Britain, with over 22% of the UK market, and analysts were holding the firm and its methods up as an object lesson in corporate success. Miquel's view is that Bell's conquest of the UK market came about as a direct consequence of the company's two-pronged home sales policy, and particularly because of the customer's perception of Bell's as a quality product.

Of all the changes Bell's saw under Miquel the most radical was the decision to take the company public in 1971. As a private company Bell's had 8 million shares in circulation, of which 69% were owned by the Gannochy Trust, and as early as March 1969 Farquharson, with a great deal of persuasion from Miquel, was hinting at a possible public issue. The following end of year saw sales up from £24 million to £27 million against a downward industry trend, and by February 1970 when Miquel conducted his first Managing Director's press conference at London's Hilton Hotel, the Press were all confidently predicting a launch some time later that year despite problems with the export trade.

The logic behind the launch was obvious. As one would expect from a business builder, Miquel believes passionately in investment, and his appointment as deputy managing director in 1965 coincided with the beginning of an enormous programme of expansion, as production volume followed the upward curve of the sales graph. It was vital to ensure sufficient stocks of whisky to meet the anticipated demand, and the company's overdraft with the Bank of Scotland now exceeded £20 million. Therefore capital was needed to maintain Bell's development programme.

The flotation, in November 1971, was extremely successful. The offer price for each 50p share was 130p, capitalising the company at £16.5 million, but six months later shares were rated at 206p, helped by an excellent set of results which saw pre-tax profits up 49% to £1.58 million. The Gannochy Trust's holding in the company fell to 49% at the time of the launch, although this was still more than adequate to secure the company against hostile bids. The proceeds of the issue were £3.1 million and with this fresh capital Miquel built extra storage facilities at Halbeath and Inchgower and began to plan another bottling hall at Dunfermline, to be built on the same model as East Mains.

Farquharson took a very great interest in the Gannochy Trust, and even when he began to relinquish his grip on the company to his protégé, he continued to guard his trusteeship jealously. The relations between companies and their charities can be complex, and it may well be that Farquharson felt it better not to have too much overlap between the two boards, but with hindsight this was a mistake that would have bitter consequences for the company. Farquharson wanted and even encouraged the rapid development of Bell's under Miquel, but his protective affection for Gannochy led him consistently to duck his successor's attempts to establish a relationship with the Board. Thus it was that when Farquharson died two years after Bell's went to the market in 1971, the link between Gannochy and Bell's management was severed and the Trust, which had an initial 49% of the new public company, began slowly to dispose of its shares.

Miquel's neighbour at his home in Gleneagles at that time was Aoinghais MacDonald, the well-respected chief general manager of insurance company General Accident whose offices were a few minutes' walk from Cherrybank. Miquel knew that the investment department of GA supported Perth companies as they had held an interest in Matthew Gloag (Grouse Scotch Whisky) before it was sold to the Highland Distilleries Company. He therefore arranged a meeting to ask MacDonald if his company would support Bell's by acquiring some of the shares which the Gannochy Trust was selling. GA agreed to do so and gradually acquired 12% of the company's equity, which was to prove vital in the Guinness takeover. This holding was considered 'friendly' and the directors of the respective companies would meet twice a year, as Bell's also conducted all its insurance business with GA. Many of the remainder of the shares ended up in the hands of institutions, some Scottish, some not, but many with little interest in Bell's other than as an investment.

The values A.K. brought to the company did not depart along with the Gannochy Trust's shareholding. Miquel maintained and then extended the company tradition of support for good causes, and in addition to cultivating a relationship with Trade charities he saw to it that Bell's was a good and generous neighbour in Perth and a kindly benefactor further afield. He could – and did – justify every penny spent in terms of promotion, brand image and goodwill, but the benefactions of the Gannochy Trust and Bell's also gave the company a reputation for social responsibility enviable in any industry, let alone in a business whose product has such potential for negative publicity.

One of the more pressing problems Miquel planned to resolve with the company's new capital was the matter of its head office. Bell's had long outgrown the Victoria Street premises from which it had operated for 70 years, and though there was room on the old site to expand this would not address the problem of old-fashioned facilities and cramped offices in the current buildings. Miquel wanted the firm to take a pride in its history, but he also wanted a headquarters that reflected the company's increasing status as a major player in a modern industry. Most of all he wanted an open-plan working environment, believing firmly that the cramped offices, corridors and closed doors at Victoria Street hindered the team culture he was determined to build into Bell's, and it became clear that if the company required such a facility in Perth, it would have to build it.

In 1972 Miquel identified a very promising site for the new head office, a derelict transport cafe which occupied an extreme corner of the city's South Inch. It had been something of an eyesore for a long time and when Bell's expressed an interest in clearing and redeveloping the site the local council was at first cautiously welcoming. The North and South Inches are ancient parkland, however, and have been regarded for centuries as hallowed ground. When the citizens of Perth read of the plan in the local press they were up in arms at the threat to their historic green belt area, so when Miquel approached the council with an alternative option, a ten-acre site under council ownership, they were so keen to sell to Bell's that they did not check the new site's previous ownership. The land in question, in Perth's Cherrybank, was an ideal location for the proposed head office since it would become the first building seen by visitors as they entered the city. The Cherrybank plot had in fact been gifted to the town by the family of Dewar's Scotch Whisky, who had intended it to be used for housing development. Lord Forteviot, the chairman of Dewar's, had to pass the site every evening on his way home from work and when he saw building activity in progress he naturally assumed that the housing project was under way. He was therefore mortified when a large sign reading 'Bell's Scotch Whisky' appeared atop the finished building, and created havoc with the council. It was all to no avail, and it was subsequently rumoured that he rerouted his homeward journey to avoid passing the new Bell's headquarters. The company, however, was more than happy with the completed Cherrybank complex, which provided all the advantages Miquel had intended. The new £320,000 Head Office opened in 1973, and within weeks of the move Miquel inherited the chairmanship on Farquharson's death.

The opening of Cherrybank, perhaps more than any other single occasion, marked the final phase of Bell's transition from small firm to major player in a modern market. It was designed by a firm of Edinburgh architects who incorporated many of Miquel's own ideas into the plan to produce a tailor-made building whose design encouraged efficient working in a pleasant environment for its 60-odd occupants. The directors' accommodation was on the top floor, away from the distractions of the administrative offices, and was served by a secretariat in a central open-plan position. The pleasant ten-acre site,

The arrival of the Duke of Edinburgh at Cherrybank in 1980.

just two miles from the centre of Perth, was carefully landscaped in what was to be the first step towards the celebrated Cherrybank gardens, although the company's Hospitality Centre was not built until some years later.

Staff transferred to Cherrybank in 1973 but the official opening did not take place until the Duke of Edinburgh's visit on July 3 1980, a red-letter day for the firm which was filmed for 'Whicker In Bell's World'. Flying directly into the grounds by helicopter, Prince Philip unveiled three plaques, to commemorate the opening not only of Cherrybank and its brand-new Reception Centre, but also of the Perth Lawn Tennis Club, recently rebuilt and now supported by the company. A special lunch in the Boardroom on the top floor was served faultlessly by the executive secretaries, who had been off to a top local hotel for a crash course in silver-service waitressing. The only hitch in the proceedings came early on, when the Duke picked up one of the three wooden pepper-mills on the table and attempted to season his smoked salmon, only to discover that whilst someone had thoughtfully positioned it within his reach, they had not got around to put the peppercorns in. 'You're pulling my leg!' he quipped to Miquel. All went smoothly thereafter, and following lunch the Duke toured the offices and Reception Centre and met a party of retired licensees. His two-and-a-half-hour visit ended with a trip to the Tennis Club, where he watched local children enjoying a regular coaching session with Jimmy MacKechnie, Bell's new Recreation Officer. Prince Philip expressed great interest and approval at the company's support for children's sporting activities. It was a happy day for all, and in addition to underlining Bell's position at the leading edge of the Scotch whisky industry the Duke's visit also showed that persistence and attention to detail were instrumental in its success. It was shortly after the Duke's visit, in 1981, that Raymond Miquel was awarded his CBE.

To reflect the company's interest in community sport, a piece of handsome silverware named the Arthur Bell Trophy was commissioned and presented by Bell's to the CCPR for it to award annually to the organisation or individual identified as having made an outstanding contribution to community sport. The trophy was handed over to the CCPR President, Prince Philip, by Miquel on

Miquel handing over the Arthur Bell Trophy to Prince Philip.

26 November 1985 at a function at the London Stock Exchange. In 1998 the presentation was made to Lady Howell, whose late husband was honoured shortly after his death for his tremendous contribution to sport in the United Kingdom.

The firm's rapid growth during the seventies soon attracted the attention of analysts and Miquel became a familiar figure first in the Scottish and business press, and then on radio and TV programmes. He never turned down a request for an interview, seeing them as part of his policy of maximum publicity for minimal outlay, and the combination of his very definite views on business and the company's success meant that he was regularly approached by journalists seeking a good quote, or wishing to profile the controversial head of this undeniably successful firm.

The tone of such interviews tends to be admiring but cautious. Many of his interviewers focused on Bell's expectations of its staff, which were undoubtedly high. In an era of industrial unrest and an increasingly casual approach to work, they were intrigued by a company whose managers worked a twelve-hour day and where sloppy dress and attitudes were simply not tolerated. Some were hostile to the company ethos – on one occasion the Secretary of State for Scotland, visiting the Dunfermline bottling hall, was asked by a waiting journalist what he thought of 'the slave-driving at this factory'. The Minister equivocated, but Miquel responded in characteristic blunt style. 'We're not slave-driving here, we're working,' he told the reporter. 'Your problem is, you've forgotten what it is like to see people working.' To others who questioned the Bell's regime he pointed out that he personally worked longer hours than anyone else, that his people were rewarded extremely well for their efforts (Bell's executive salaries averaged 20-40% higher than those of its competitors, and the firm provided free meals, transport and pensions for its employees) and that the hard work was a team effort anyway. Despite these arguments some commentators never accepted that the Bell's regime was a fair one and continued to criticise the company for its 'paternalistic' attitude, but others recognised that its management style was the essential reason why the company had prospered despite the recession. The well-known Scottish MP Nicholas Fairbairn, in his newspaper column, described Miquel's style as 'hard and humane at work and responsible to the community,' summing up the Bell's philosophy in a single sentence. The long hours sometimes paid valuable dividends. Anyone phoning Bell's late on a Friday evening would be fairly sure of raising at least one of the management team, so when an Italian firm called on spec wanting to arrange a distillery visit Bell's was the only whisky firm that answered their calls and a useful contract resulted.

Nobody argued that Miquel's approach worked, but his style of leadership still came regularly under scrutiny. In fact, one of the main problems he would face in the Guinness takeover battle was the latter's portrayal of Bell's as a one-man band. As far as his management of people is concerned, Miquel has always emphatically denied this charge, retorting that critics simply fail to comprehend the broad, team-based management structure he has always favoured. For proof he cites the regular overseas trips that took him out of the country for up to three months a year during his management of Bell's; strong team management, he maintains, ensured all ran smoothly in his absence. He sees a managing director's role as that of a coach, whose overriding responsibility is to set and maintain policy and ensure that all team members are capable of working within it. The thing that makes his style effective, he believes, is his approach to the operational aspects of the firm. Far from resisting 'hands on', Miquel has spent much of his career deliberately immersing himself in the detail of his companies, and accepts the long working hours as a necessary part of the package. Without knowing everything that is going on in the organisation, he says, he cannot possibly make any kind of overall assessment and decision, and is likely to miss opportunities. Few chief executives will find time to do this, preferring to rely on a pyramidal management structure and reporting system; Miquel is dismissive of this easy option. 'There's a lot said about delegation in industry, but I believe a manager needs to understand the product and the subject inside out, and give the job in hand his or her undivided attention.'

To illustrate the value he set on teamwork Miquel was able to point to the 600 free shares issued to all employees each year. This unusually democratic scheme meant that a worker on the bottling line could expect exactly the same number of shares per year as the chairman himself, and long-term employees built up substantial holdings.

During the takeover battle in 1985 the value of most individuals' holdings amounted to around £24,000. Those who chose to hold on to their shares – and many did – were still able to benefit from them, using them for example as security for bank loans on the advice of the company's own bank, and thus all Bell's employees had access to far more financial options than were enjoyed by their counterparts in most other similar companies. The benevolent ghost of A.K. Bell would have approved of the share issue, but Raymond Miquel saw it simply as common sense to give the firm's workers a stake in its success. Twenty years before the phrase 'stakeholder society' was coined Bell's was among the few companies which gave all employees, whatever their status, the opportunity to gain directly from their own productivity.

CHAPTER 4

Expanding Horizons –
the Bell's Group of Companies

IN EARLY 1973 BELL'S, in common with other drinks manufacturers, was experiencing problems with the supply of bottles. Severe shortages in the UK market forced it to go to the continent where prices were higher, and Bell's was not the only company to look around for a solution closer to home. The firm was still reasonably well off following flotation and had been seriously considering expansion by acquisition, so now the possibility was mooted that it might purchase its way out of the current supply problems.

Canning Town Glass was a glassmaking company with factories on the Isle of Sheppey, south of London and Mexborough in Yorkshire. Bell's had been customers for seven years, and 40% of its bottles were now sourced from Canning Town, so when the opportunity to purchase an interest in the company arose in April, the company was an obvious target. Profits in 1972 had been £174,000, although the half-year figures for 1973 had shown a loss of £41,000 which was a cause for concern, and explained the low share price of around 40p. Canning Town's departing chairman was Lord Brayley, who had just been ennobled by the Labour government and appointed as an Under-Secretary for Defence, and who had resigned from the company as a consequence and put his family's 25% holding up for sale. Over previous years Bell's had acquired a small number of shares in its supplier on the open market and the purchase of Lord Brayley's holding now gave it 1.37 million shares, which represented just under 30% of the company. Raymond Miquel was appointed chairman of Bell's new investment.

It quickly became apparent that all was not well. The company's surprisingly poor performance in previous months had no obvious cause, and when an investigation was launched the auditors soon found a large hole in the company's finances linked to the 'Towmaster' account. The latter sounded grand, but was in fact a single tractor and trailer unit used by the company to deliver bottles around the London area. Questions were asked about sums that appeared to have gone out via this account and Miquel contacted Lord Brayley for an urgent meeting regarding the irregularities. Lord Brayley agreed, and a private room was taken at the Churchill Hotel in Portman Square, where he arrived at the appointed time in a staff car with flags flying, a privilege to which his new position in the Wilson government entitled him. The partner in the accountants auditing Canning Town was present, as were Miquel and the managing director of the glass company.

Lord Brayley admitted taking money from the company, and after a great deal of negotiation between him and Miquel he agreed to pay £143,000 within two weeks to clear the sums involved. This would enable Canning Town to complete its accounts in time for the company's AGM. They shook hands on the deal, but unfortunately the auditor had his firm's lawyer contact Miquel to advise that they believed the transaction might not be legal. Bell's sought Queen's Counsel's opinion and they were advised to qualify the Canning Town accounts for the AGM in September 1973 and instruct the accountants to make further investigations. Miquel was furious; £143,000 seemed a fair settlement for the sums of money that Lord Brayley had admitted withdrawing from the company. However, he was advised that the settlement might not be in the shareholders' best interests, as other amounts might have been taken out in previous years.

The year-end results were due to be published in August, so time was vital if a public row was to be avoided, but a few weeks of urgent consultation failed to produce a suitable compromise. On Monday September 9 Miquel arrived at the Piccadilly offices to conduct the AGM. One shareholder was in attendance, along with some thirty journalists, who faced Miquel, the managing director of Canning Town Glass and four lawyers at the top table. The matter was a political hot potato for the Wilson government and the shareholder had been well primed by the Press to ask the questions. 'It was the only AGM I have ever conducted when the answers had to be cleared by a lawyer before I could respond.'

The affair was an unpleasant one. Lord Brayley was dishonoured and Canning Town had to pick up the pieces under the chairmanship of Miquel. After two years of investigations the accountants had been able to establish that over £500,000 might have been taken from the company, as a result of which the taxman reclaimed £150,000 from it in unpaid taxes. The accountants' and lawyers' bill came to £200,000, and it was left to Canning Town Glass to take out a case against Lord Brayley to reclaim costs. By this time the company had paid out £350,000 and had not received the £143,000 from Lord Brayley as originally agreed. Lord Brayley died with very little money, and Canning Town and its shareholders were worse off by £493,000 thanks to the wisdom of the law. The whole episode sat uneasily with Miquel. 'I'm convinced it was not the right decision. Integrity is so important in business, and when you see people getting away with sharp practice, it demeans business as a whole. It left a nasty taste, particularly the dealings with lawyers and accountants as the whole affair seemed to have political undertones.'

Canning Town Glass is a good example of Bell's policies at work outside the firm. Originally an investment intended to solve a short-term supply problem, Bell's 30% share of Canning Town became a controlling interest in 1975 when it bought the company, and despite early financial problems it continued to support and develop its investment. The Isle of Sheppey factory provided work for over 300 people in a deprived area and Miquel decided to invest in new plant to ensure its long-term future. When Norman Tebbit (now Lord Tebbit), the Trade and Industry Minister in Mrs Thatcher's government opened the new furnace and production line there in 1984, their jobs appeared secure. Bell's invested over £11 million in Canning Town Glass between 1975 and 1984, and thanks to this investment over 900 jobs were secured and the company was well equipped to compete in an increasingly difficult market, attracting business from many sources – it was, for example, the biggest supplier of milk bottles in the UK. Nor did Towmaster fare badly under its new owners. Miquel thought it was an excellent name and the single vehicle became the starting point for a small fleet of lorries which began to replace outside contractors for Bell's transport needs. By 1984 Towmaster had four main depots in the UK and 125 vehicles

Norman Tebbit, Minister of State for Trade and Industry, performs the official opening of the new Furnace and Manufacturing Complex at Canning Town.

and despite its small beginnings and high start-up costs, the fleet was showing signs of becoming a useful asset indeed.

Bell's had remained in good shape despite the more difficult trading conditions in the Scotch whisky industry in the early 1980s, a fact not lost on market analysts who regularly noted the firm's potential as a takeover prospect. Profits in 1982 hit a record high of £31.2 million, up £3.5 million on the previous year despite disappointing results from Canning Town Glass, and the company had cash reserves of around £30 million due to good cash-flow from profits, improved stock control techniques and the completion of several major building projects. In this respect Bell's was in a much better position than many of its competitors. Miquel had always spoken of his willingness to diversify provided the product was right, and as the firm looked to crack the US barrier and develop new markets for its traditional business, it seemed fitting that it should widen the scope of its activities.

The firm's experience of takeovers had been mixed. Quite apart from the particular difficulties of Canning Town and Towmaster, it is a fact that a company like Arthur Bell, whose management style and structure are instrumental to its success, faces particular difficulties in bringing an entirely different organisation into the charmed circle, and sometimes a great deal of shaking and trimming is needed before a fit is achieved. Overall, though, the purchase and development of these enterprises had given Bell's management firsthand experience of the process of acquisition. Bell's had been seen to make a success of a takeover, and its acquisitions so far had generally been perceived by commentators as positive and well chosen to fit in with their existing business.

During this period, and at the express wish of Robert Maxwell, Miquel and Lord Spens were invited to meet him for a discussion that he said would be mutually beneficial. It was agreed to fit in a 7.15 a.m. breakfast meeting at his office, 'Maxwell House', and when they arrived they were instructed to take a lift to the top floor. A butler met them at the lift doors and directed them into a private lounge area. To Miquel's surprise, Robert Maxwell entered the room in a silk dressing-gown and took them through to a dining area. It was not what one would call a business meeting; however, during the breakfast Maxwell stated that he would like Bell's to acquire a 49% share of the equity of the *Scottish Daily Record*. He suggested that Miquel would become chairman of the company and Maxwell would retain a 51% shareholding. Whilst the offer was inviting Miquel explained that if Bell's was to consider the proposal, it would have to have 100% ownership. Maxwell, although interested in the cash, did not want to lose control so after a lengthy discussion the breakfast was completed without any agreement to move his proposal forward.

In 1980 Miquel was approached by Sir Alan Smith, chairman & chief executive of Dawson's International (owners of Pringle and other famous knitwear brands) to become a non-executive director on his board. He explained the company's operation and, as Miquel admired the way Sir Alan had built up Dawson's and felt he could make a contribution, he accepted the appointment in early 1981. During his two years with the company he visited all the group's various manufacturing companies with Sir Alan and made several recommendations, some of which were adopted. What appeared strange to Miquel at the time was that there was not a Group Marketing Director, and the managing director of each of the subsidiary companies was responsible for his own advertising spend in developing the brands. The managing directors were each paid a bonus on the annual profit made by their company, and this was a disincentive for them to spend money on promotional activity.

Late in 1982, having witnessed the way Dawson's products were marketed overseas and convinced that the total promotional spend was inadequate to develop sales of the famous knitwear brands, Miquel became interested in forming close ties between Bell's and Dawsons. They were two strong, independent quality Scottish companies and he felt that to merge the companies would enable Bell's world network of key overseas sales executives to be used to further the development of the Dawson brands. Bell's and Dawson's would create a strong Scottish company with two of the country's premier brands in Bell's Scotch Whisky and Pringle knitwear. Stanley Fields was chairman of William Baird, which owned 27% of Dawson's equity, and he was a non-executive director of Dawson's. He supported Miquel's ideas and indicated that Baird would be willing to pass its 27% to Bell's if there was to be a takeover bid. Miquel made it quite clear to Stanley Fields that Bell's would only proceed with a takeover if Sir Alan was agreeable to the proposals.

It was decided that they should arrange a breakfast meeting in London with Sir Alan and Bell's merchant bankers, to discuss the proposition. Sir Alan was unaware of the reason for the early-morning discussion, and when the subject was eventually raised he was not particularly receptive, but asked Miquel what his position would be after the merger. 'Deputy chairman,' was the reply, to which Sir Alan responded: 'I have been chairman and chief executive of my company for decades, and I am not about to become a deputy.' The discussions ended there, and on his return to Perth Miquel met Sir Alan to discuss his position with Dawson's. Sir Alan was keen to forget the incident and requested that Miquel remain on the Dawson's board, but Miquel felt something of a Judas for having discussed the acquisition possibilities with Stanley Fields without Sir Alan's knowledge, and felt he had no option but to resign.

The Dawson's incident illustrates Bell's measured approach to the business of takeovers and Miquel's reluctance to fight an underhand or destructive battle. His advisers, Morgan Grenfell, were instructed to remain alert for a company which could be integrated into the Bell's fold and a year later they brought to his attention one business in particular: the Gleneagles Hotel Group. It would fit comfortably into Bell's existing operations, but was not suffering the particular hardships of their own industry. A quality business, it would sit comfortably with the Bell's brand whose image Miquel and others had striven so assiduously to develop and protect. And, in keeping with Bell's commitment to Scotland, its flagship brand was a byword for Scottish excellence.

In January 1981, as part of Conservative reform of the railways, British Transport Hotels was forcibly 'privatised'. Three large, prestigious Scottish hotels – the Caledonian and the North British in Edinburgh and the high-profile Gleneagles – were sold for a total of £13.5m to form the Gleneagles Hotel Group in a deal arranged by the British Linen Bank, an investment arm of the Bank of Scotland, the purchase being funded by the issue of 9 million £1 shares and £4.5m of loan stock. Around a third of the issue was taken up by British Transport Hotels, whose advisers were Morgan Grenfell, and who thus became the majority shareholder with the remainder going to various Scottish businessmen, institutional investors and pension funds. The new firm was young, thrusting and enthusiastically independent, and concentrated on building up the Group – especially the Gleneagles Hotel – into a vibrant and viable proposition, and this at a time of international recession, when many believed the newly privatised hotels could never show a profit. Peter Tyrie, the young managing director brought in to run the firm, looked forward confidently to a period of expansion and growth as Gleneagles established itself as a credible contender in the UK luxury hotel league. The Gleneagles Group's first move out of Scotland was to take a 125-year lease on London's Piccadilly Hotel, which had an excellent site and enormous potential. It would need considerable refurbishment, however, if it was to come up to the Group's standards and function as a London flagship. The Board proposed a rights issue to raise the £9.7m needed to complete the refurbishment, and an extraordinary board meeting was scheduled at the Caledonian Hotel for Wednesday January 11th 1984, when everyone would have returned from the Christmas break.

This was a large step for the fledgling hotel group and the markets would certainly see it as a risk. Despite Gleneagles' profit forecasts of around £1 million for 1983, some investors felt that their funds might be more secure elsewhere and British Transport Hotels decided to reduce its large holding in the company. Morgan Grenfell, the merchant bank charged with the disposal, was well aware of Bell's interest in strong Scottish brands; it had acted for Bell's for some years and regularly reported to Miquel on possible acquisitions. Now it suggested to Miquel that Bell's might be interested in taking up this substantial block of Gleneagles shares.

Seeing the changes Tyrie had made at Gleneagles, Miquel was impressed. He recognised something of himself in the younger man, another fitness enthusiast with a reputation as a demanding, hardworking employer, and, like Miquel, a manager who believed in investment for growth. Gleneagles' profits for 1982 had been a modest £83,000 on a turnover of £8.2 million, thanks to an ambitious development programme, but the latter had promoted the hotels into a different league and their new popularity promised a swift return on the investment. The matchmaking was successful and just before Christmas Eve 1983 Bell's secured the majority of BTH's holding in the Gleneagles Group – 29.9% – for 225p per share. For BTH this had been an irresistible offer, more than doubling the value of its initial £3m investment in just 18 months, and leaving it with a 3% stake in Gleneagles. With that one handshake Bell's had acquired a substantial slice of the company before the board had even heard about the bid, and Miquel might be forgiven for allowing himself a small dram of his own product as he left to spend the festive season with his family.

News of Miquel's coup broke on 4 January when Bell's launched a formal bid for the Gleneagles Group. The offer terms – 173 new Bell's shares for every 100 Gleneagles or 225p cash, valuing the company at £20.2m – were well received by the markets. Indeed, Bell's shares actually rose a little at the news, an unusual outcome for a company launching a takeover bid, and implying that the move was viewed as a shrewd one. The Gleneagles board, however, opposed Bell's bid emphatically, rejected the valuation and hurriedly set about preparing a defence, a task made more difficult by the City. Bell's strategy was praised by commentators including the FT's own Lex, who also pointed out that Gleneagles' proposed rights price of 135p hardly supported the latter's claims of a gross undervaluation. Much was made of the Piccadilly commitment, and Bell's made it clear that they saw grave implications for shareholders if the rights issue went ahead.

In fact, Gleneagles' major problem in rallying its shareholders was not so much nervousness over the Piccadilly project as the persuasiveness of Bell's arguments in favour of a merger. Bell's had sufficient resources to fund reasonable growth from within, and some experience of the hospitality business. It was an independent, successful Scottish company, so deeply committed to the region that it had never even opened a London office, whose product represented the very essence of Scottish quality. What better partner for the Gleneagles brand? Furthermore, it was whispered, the Kuwait Investment Office held a 15% stake in the group already and was known for its ability to spot a good opportunity. Surely Gleneagles should remain Scottish, even under Bell's umbrella, rather than fall to foreigners so early in its renaissance?

The Gleneagles board worked hard to counter these arguments. Ironically enough, Gleneagles' chairman was Sir Alan Smith, with whom Miquel had his ill-fated discussions the previous year concerning a possible merger between Bell's and Dawson's International. Sir Alan urged Gleneagles' shareholders to reject the bid but had to admit a personal respect for Bell's chairman, describing him as 'hard-working – and impossible.' Nevertheless, the firm's defence grew increasingly desperate and when Raymond Miquel was photographed outside the Gleneagles Hotel for a TV profile the group protested angrily to the Takeover Panel, suggesting that because the programme was due to go out the day before the first closing date it might have an influence on the outcome. The programme was in fact unrelated to the bid, but the suggestion that Bell's was resorting to dirty tricks was seen to suggest growing anxiety in the Gleneagles camp.

The first bid closed on 26 January 1984 and Bell's immediately made an improved offer of 100 for 100. This quickly secured the remainder of the important institutionals, including the British Linen

Bank, Coats Patons and Distillers, as well as BTH's remaining 3%. By 27 January Arthur Bell held 52.24% of the company.

Miquel admits to some sentimentality in Bell's bid for Gleneagles. His home for the past thirty years lies a few hundred yards from the Gleneagles Hotel entrance and he has an enormous affection for the great building, which he has seen over the years both in decline and at its best. 'There were rumours that the Kuwait Investment Office wanted it,' he says, 'and I hated the idea of a Scottish business like that being run at arms' length by a foreign concern. I knew we could do it better. I really wanted Gleneagles to be part of Bell's . . . I thought it was an ideal match.' As soon as the takeover was complete he became chairman of Gleneagles and launched himself into the task of bringing the companies together, a job that required him to secure the co-operation of Gleneagles' staff and management.

After the takeover of Gleneagles an account and invoice were received from Quayle Munro, who had acted as advisers to Gleneagles during the takeover. The fee for their services had been agreed with Gleneagles' board at £300,000 if they were successful in fending off Bell's – or £600,000 if they failed. It was the first time Miquel had seen a fee doubled for failure and to him it said something about the City and the integrity of the people concerned. Bell's did take up the matter with its legal advisers, but they were advised to settle the account.

Miquel doesn't believe in regrets, and has never lost sleep over what might have been. He believes this trait comes from his love of sport – 'I learned early on how to win and to lose,' he remarks, 'and to put the game behind you and move on.' This resilience has seen him through difficult times, from which he has emerged with his energy undiminished and his appetite for business as keen as ever. Perhaps the nearest he comes to a rueful shake of the head is when he considers his decision after the takeover to promote Peter Tyrie to the board of Bell's. Any disappointment he feels, however, is more for the company's sake, in the light of subsequent events. It is no secret that Miquel thought that in Tyrie he had perhaps found his eventual successor. 'If Bell's had not been acquired by Guinness, he might have had everything he was looking for and more, particularly if Bell's bid for Westin Hotels in the USA had been able to proceed.' Never dwelling on the past himself, he hoped Tyrie, as a good manager, would put the bitterness of the Gleneagles takeover behind him and make the most of the opportunities offered by his new role.

'What was said during the takeover doesn't mean a thing,' he told a press conference at the time. 'The fellow probably did the sort of thing I would do. I've only known him three months but I like his approach, his attitudes and his enthusiasm.' Taking these reasons into account Miquel offered Tyrie the chance to stay on and appointed him a director of Bell's, and the new management team settled down to work under a flag of truce. Miquel was convinced that integration could be achieved swiftly and with relatively little upheaval, and when Peter Tyrie donned shorts and singlet and battled him step for step in the firm's annual sports day the following June, he felt that an important milestone had been passed.

The sixteen months following the Gleneagles takeover were amongst the most progressive, professionally and personally, of

Scottish Secretary of State, George Younger, opens the £950,000 top floor of bedrooms at Gleneagles Hotel in 1984 which marked the completion of a £5 million refurbishment programme.

Raymond Miquel's career. Once Gleneagles was secured the firm began to apply the Bell's touch to its new acquisitions, and it was satisfying for Miquel to see the extra polish on the hotel operations which was the hallmark of the parent company. Peter Tyrie continued to head the Hotels division, and he and Miquel were usually in agreement on most matters of operational policy. Perhaps the most telling disagreement they had came in September 1984, when Miquel returned from a business trip to discover that at short notice Tyrie had agreed to hold the first Dunhill Golf Cup at Gleneagles the following month.

Miquel had not been consulted and he was totally opposed to the idea. The weather in Scotland is not at all good in October and the scenery is past its best, so it would be a highly unwise time to promote the Gleneagles Hotel and golf courses on national and international television. Miquel advised Tyrie that he should tell Dunhill to find another venue. This brought an immediate telephone call from Tony Greener, the managing director of Dunhill, who tried to persuade him to change his mind. Miquel, however, remained adamant that Gleneagles could not host the tournament. The promoter was Mark McCormack's International Management Group (IMG) and Miquel then received a call from McCormack, who was in the USA. After Miquel explained, Mark accepted the situation and the Dunhill Cup went to St Andrews. Mark McCormack bore no grudge over the incident; he has remained a friend of Miquel's since that day and the two occasionally meet at Gleneagles.

Meanwhile there was a breakthrough in the whisky business. Bell's had made many attempts to get a foothold in the US market over the years but success had always proved elusive. One problem was the product's premium image on price in a market dominated by cheap, high-profile domestic brands, and another was the complex legalities of importing liquor into the States which meant that foreign brands could not get onto the US market except through a US importer and from there on to a State distributor. Miquel replaced Heublein, which had been Bell's importers since the 1950s, with Jim Beam in 1969, but after ten years of little progress he appointed Monsieur Henri Wines, a subsidiary of PepsiCo, to perform this function. They developed a small niche market presence but without an agent under its direct control Bell's would never be able to apply its successful formula to the venture. The company needed to buy its own American importer to develop its sales, as Miquel knew this was the obvious route to any chance of a meaningful share of the lucrative US whisky market. His numerous visits to America over the years had always included meetings with State distributors and many retail calls, and therefore he had a fair knowledge of what was required. Finally in February 1984, after a series of patient negotiations, he struck gold. Bell's bought Wellington Importers, a wine and spirit operation based in New York, and in the four months between the acquisition and the financial year-end on 30 June the company contributed £177,000 to Group profits.

Since the mid-1970s Bell's American operation had been headed up by an ex-vice president of sales in Jim Beam called Herb Kanter. He was a keen sportsman and an excellent salesman and after the Wellington acquisition he and Miquel developed plans to establish the brand as a leader in the marketplace. Over the years a network of 22 State distributors had been appointed to cover sales in all major markets in the USA and regular meetings and presentations were made to each distributor. This resulted in considerable sales progress in several states before the Guinness takeover in September 1985.

Miquel can recall that he and Kanter visited distributors after the takeover, in November 1985, and made several retail calls to analyse the distribution and merchandising of the Bell's brand. While he was doing this, he decided to include the merchandising of Guinness. When two weeks later he met Ernest Saunders in New York and reported his findings, which were positive regarding Bell's but showed very little distribution of the Guinness brand, Saunders' only reaction was to say: 'Raymond, I think you should go to Malaysia; you could do a good job for us there.' Within months of the Guinness takeover the US operation was closed down and any chance of Bell's establishing itself in the US market had gone forever.

A postscript to the USA affair seems to be summed up in a letter Miquel received in January 1986, after the takeover, from Howard Jacobs, president of Reitman Industries, a distributor in New Jersey, which stated: 'One of the great pleasures of business is to meet professionals in all its phases. When I think of the consummate

With Herb Kanter (right) and Perry Como at the official reception for the 1983 Ryder Cup in Florida.

professional, I think of you. Your dynamism and creativity are at work 24 hours a day. There is no doubt in my mind or my associates' that you will be a success at whatever task you attempt and it was a pleasure being part of your efforts to build Bell's, here in the United States.'

The spring of 1984 had seen further developments at Perth, with work starting on an ambitious new scheme. After a great deal of discussion with the Provost of Perth and the local council, Bell's was able to purchase a six-acre site adjacent to the pitch-and-putt course and gardens around the Bell's head office. The idea was to further extend and develop Bell's Cherrybank gardens, to include a collection of fine sculptures by Scottish artists, a variety of heathers, a children's swing park, an aviary and other features. The gardens would be open to the public and would attract a great deal of local interest. Each December a Christmas tree and an illuminated animal display were featured in the gardens and were again extremely popular. A valuable resource to the company, which now entertained thousands of visitors at Cherrybank, the gardens also maintained Bell's links with the community. A trust was established in 1985, chaired by Miquel, with the objective of providing facilities for social welfare and recreation for Perth and its citizens via the gardens, and this would ensure their care and maintenance in perpetuity, or so he thought. In February 1987, over a year after he left the company, Miquel received a letter from Bell's company secretary. The gardens' Declaration of Trust, it explained, stated that the appointment of trustees was vested solely in Arthur Bell & Sons. Since Miquel was no longer a director of Bell's he was not eligible to be a trustee and the letter asked for his resignation. After the receipt of assurances from Guinness that the gardens would be completed and remain open to the public, Miquel agreed to resign in favour of John Mathieson, the then Provost of Perth.

On a personal note 1984 also saw recognition of Miquel's management expertise by the academic world. In October of that year he was approached by Professor David Weir, head of Glasgow University's Business School, who wished to propose Miquel for a visiting professorship. The reactionary in Miquel loved the idea of influencing the managers of the future; he has always believed in the importance of education and training but makes no secret of his impatience with a system that can equip an individual with theory and jargon, but instil no appreciation of the commitment needed to put their knowledge to use. Despite his own experience of further education, or perhaps because of it, he values practical experience and good on-the-job training just as highly as paper qualifications. Not that he is suspicious of bright young graduates – on the contrary, he is well known for promoting youngsters quickly where they show promise, even to Board level when appropriate. He likes working with a young team, he says: 'Their attitudes are less fixed than those of older people. They don't think they know everything, and they can be trained to do things the way you want them done.' The university awarded few such professorships but after discussions with Professor Weir Miquel received a formal offer from the University Court and became a non-stipendiary Visiting Professor in Business Development in May 1985, a role he has continued to fill ever since, also sitting as a member of the University of Glasgow Business School's advisory board. It was a far cry from the long evenings he had once spent studying marketing and accountancy after a full day's work at Leith and a long drive back to Glasgow, with the prospect of a ten-mile training run ahead of him and an early start the next morning.

Towards the end of 1984 Miquel had conducted lengthy negotiations with Wilson Sporting Goods, a subsidiary company of PepsiCo, who were keen to divest themselves of this investment. The New York merchant bank Dillon Read & Co., along with Lord Spens of Ansbacher, was acting on behalf of Bell's and had virtually agreed an acceptable price of $143 million. On 23 February 1985 Miquel and Bell's non-executive director Henry King, who was also the company lawyer, met in New York to thrash out the problem of Wilson's 2000 employees, who were part of the PepsiCo pension scheme. Although Miquel had analysed the worldwide Wilson operation and identified many potential opportunities with the Wilson management, who seemed keen to work under the Bell's regime, he was advised by the lawyers not to get involved in transferring pensions as this could prove very expensive under US legislation. PepsiCo did not want Wilson's employees to remain in their scheme, so this did appear to be a stumbling block. Nevertheless Bell's made an offer in February 1985 on the basis that benefits accrued in the PepsiCo pension scheme would remain and Bell's would take responsibility for pensions from the date of acquisition. On 20 May Bell's was officially advised by PepsiCo that it had accepted an unconditional offer from another company, Wesray. Had the acquisition proceeded there is no doubt that the enlarged Bell's firm would have been completely out of the reach of Guinness.

Westin Hotels in the USA was owned by the troubled United Airlines and in 1984 it was looking to divest itself of the hotels division. Miquel saw this as an opportunity to develop the group of Gleneagles Hotels. He was familiar with the prestigious hotels owned by Westin, having always stayed at the Century Plaza in Los Angeles, the Westin Hotel (formerly the Continental Plaza) in Chicago, and the Plaza Hotel in New York during his visits to the United States. These five-star hotels were all part of the Westin group and seemed a suitable fit for Bell's hotels division. Miquel's initial meeting was with Ken Mallory, vice-president of Westin, who discussed Bell's interest with Harry Mullikin, the chairman and chief executive. Both were keen to pursue the proposals and sent various financial papers detailing information on the hotels group. A further meeting was held in New York on 16 May 1985 with Dwight Call, president of Westin Hotels, when Henry King, Bell's lawyer was present. It was agreed that the parties would meet again on 25 June in New York after an on-site inspection of the Gleneagles Hotels by a small and discreet team from Westin. Unfortunately events overtook these arrangements – the Guinness bid for Bell's came through on 13 June and the New York meeting had to be cancelled. On 18 June Ken Mallory wrote saying that they understood the reason for the cancellation but that as soon as the Guinness bid had been rebuffed Dwight Call looked forward to continuing the discussions. It was to be a good opportunity lost for the development of Gleneagles. After the takeover Guinness sold the North British and Caledonian hotels in Edinburgh and the Piccadilly Hotel in London. They only kept the Gleneagles Hotel itself and were not interested in developing the hotels division.

CHAPTER 5

The Guinness Takeover of Bell's

AT 1.30 A.M. ON FRIDAY 14 JUNE 1985 the phone rang in Raymond
Miquel's suite in the Westin Hotel, Chicago. The caller was Geoff
Cooper, Bell's finance director, and the news he brought was as
unwelcome as it was unexpected: Ernest Saunders' Guinness plc had
announced publicly that it was bidding for Bell's. The firm's
continuing success and healthy cash reserves had regularly provoked
speculation and the recent share price (currently around 160p) was
regarded as an undervaluation, but a bid was the last thing Bell's
needed at that moment, involved as it was in takeover negotiations of
its own. This was not the worst of it, however; Cooper also told
Miquel that Morgan Grenfell, Bell's own merchant bank, was advising
Guinness in its bid. Miquel gleaned from Cooper as much as he could
and then embarked on the first of a number of international
telephone calls he would make that night. His first priority was to
establish the legal position and for this he needed to reach Henry
King, the independent non-executive director on Bell's board of
seven, and a partner in Denton Hall & Burgin of London, who had
acted as the company solicitors for many years.

It took a long time to track Henry King down; he was on business
in the Far East and Miquel telephoned fruitlessly from the suite in
Chicago for some time before finally tracking the man down at 4 a.m.
in his hotel. Assuming he must be unaware of Guinness's move,
Miquel explained quickly what had happened and asked how they
should proceed.

There was a brief embarrassed silence. Then: 'Yes, I heard about it.
I'm sorry, Raymond, I can't help you.' Explanations were stilted, but
the story was simple enough. The previous year King had acted for
Saunders' wife in a private legal matter. Conflict of interests decreed
he could not get involved in the takeover battle in any way. A more
suspicious man might have wondered at this most untimely of

coincidences, particularly when King's firm, which had initially believed itself free to assist Bell's, changed its mind seven days later, forcing the company to find new legal advisers.

The role of a merchant bank in any takeover is a vital one and a company's plans can stand or fall on the expertise of its financial advisers. Morgan Grenfell had represented Bell's since 1967, handling both the 1971 flotation and the purchase of Canning Town Glass as well as more routine matters, and attending biannual press conferences to announce Bell's interim and annual results. They had also advised the company on potential UK acquisitions, including discussions with British Caledonian in 1984, and although Henry Ansbacher had represented Bell's in the unsuccessful bid for Wilson Sporting Goods in February 1985, Morgan Grenfell had been briefed on the matter at Bell's March 1985 press conference, at which they had been represented by David Ewart.

Bell's link with Henry Ansbacher was a recent one. In the summer of 1982 Lord Spens, who had handled the Bell's account at Morgan Grenfell, left the bank to become managing director of Ansbacher. Patrick Spens, a large, convivial character who had been something of a high-flyer in his younger days, had enjoyed a cordial relationship with Miquel and Bell's over the years. Miquel classed him as a friend and wished him well in his new venture but he saw every reason for Bell's business to remain with Morgan Grenfell, so Roger Seelig, a friend and previous colleague of Spens, was given responsibility for the account in his stead. Unfortunately a working relationship between Seelig and Miquel proved hard to establish. The first problem came in October 1982, when Bell's expressed concern at Morgan Grenfell's links with Seagram, a potential bidder for Bell's. Seelig reassured Bell's that there was no cause for concern, but relations continued to deteriorate and by early 1983 it was clear to Miquel that he and Seelig could not work together. On 3 February Miquel wrote to Morgan Grenfell's Chief Executive, Christopher Reeves, suggesting that in view of these difficulties Bell's would begin 'a gradual winding-down' of its relationship with the bank.

This letter brought an immediate response from Morgan Grenfell's senior management, who can hardly have been overjoyed at the prospect of losing a major client. Miquel and Geoff Cooper were invited to lunch with Reeves at the Connaught on 14 February where they met David Ewart, whom Reeves hoped Bell's would accept in Roger Seelig's place. Much was resolved during the meeting; Miquel agreed to leave Bell's UK business where it was and Ewart made plans to visit Perth on 25 February to familiarise himself with his new responsibility. A relieved Reeves wrote to Miquel the day following the meeting, expressing his conviction that much had been done to clear the air and looking forward to meeting him later that year to review progress on 'a series of most important moves' for the development of Bell's. David Ewart and his assistant director, Christopher Knight, duly took up their roles and on 23 March a strategy meeting was held at which Bell's and its bankers looked at the company's undoubted need for diversification and discussed potential acquisitions.

It is important to stress Bell's firm decision to remain with Morgan Grenfell, since it would later be suggested that from this point onwards the two went their separate ways and Bell's transferred its allegiance to Lord Spens and Ansbacher. In fact Bell's had gone out of its way to demonstrate that this was not the case. Spens and Miquel had dined together in London on Wednesday 16 February, two days after the lunch with Christopher Reeves, but the conversation had focused only on the possibility of Ansbacher's assisting Bell's in its search for a US acquisition. If Spens had hoped for more, Miquel's letter of 12 April left him in no doubt of the company's intentions:

> Regarding our involvement with Morgan Grenfell, I should point out that we have been using them as Merchant Bankers now for many years and when you left the Company and, at a subsequent meeting with Mr. Christopher Reeves, we stated that we would continue to use Morgan Grenfell in the United Kingdom.
>
> The reason we contacted you in December regarding Gleneagles Hotels PLC was because Morgan Grenfell were acting for B.T.H. and this was mentioned to you at that time.
>
> As far as our operation in the United States is concerned, we did write to you on 18th February, 1983, confirming that we would utilise the services of Henry Ansbacher & Co. Limited in the USA., therefore any acquisition in the UK should not be of concern to Ansbacher.

On a more personal note, I have always enjoyed working with you and it is regrettable that you left the employment of Morgan Grenfell. I am sure you will realise that this is not suitable justification for us to switch our merchant banking arrangements.

Bell's decision to instruct Ansbacher over the acquisition of a US distributorship had arisen out of a dissatisfaction with Morgan Grenfell's US office. Oppenheimer & McKinsey, Bell's existing US advisers on company acquisitions, had already identified a few interesting prospects when Ansbacher came into the picture, and within a couple of months Wellington Importers had emerged as a serious candidate. Unchallenged therefore in its role as Bell's UK merchant bankers, Morgan Grenfell continued to provide the company with reports on potential UK acquisitions – over the next two years it was to identify six such companies: Vere Hotels; British Caledonian; Drambuie; Dunlop; Weetabix; and James Burrough. It also carried out a general sector review of Bell's in March 1983.

Ansbacher's next major involvement with Bell's came in late 1983, when the Gleneagles takeover process began. The fact that Ansbacher acted for Bell's in this transaction would later be used to legitimise Morgan Grenfell's role as Guinness's advisers in the takeover bid. In fact, as Miquel's letter to Patrick Spens makes clear, Bell's was forced into using another merchant bank for this one UK deal because of Morgan Grenfell's existing ties to Gleneagles, and Ansbacher had understood this from the moment it was sounded out about the deal as far back as the previous December. Far from there having been any friction with Morgan Grenfell, the latter had acted as matchmaker in the Gleneagles deal; as merchant banker to British Transport Hotels Ltd it had been charged with the disposal of BTH's holding in the Gleneagles Group and promptly offered it to Bell's. This introduction seemed proof positive, if any were needed, of Morgan Grenfell's continuing concern for Bell's interests, since it set Bell's well on the way to an acquisition of the exact type the company had been discussing with the bank since the reconciliation nine months previously. Morgan Grenfell extended support and co-operation to both parties throughout the sale. Bell's acquisition of Gleneagles at the end of January 1984 had certainly been facilitated by Morgan

Grenfell's actions, and Miquel continued to regard the bank as its advisers in all UK corporate finance matters, even consulting it about a proposed reorganisation of the Group's structure in December of that year. Morgan Grenfell's comments and advice on that occasion, contained in a detailed 4-page letter from David Ewart dated 14 December 1984, demonstrated an understanding of Bell's internal workings that sits uneasily with their claim to the Takeover Panel, just six months later, that links with the firm had been severed almost two years previously.

Early coverage of the Guinness bid was mixed – there were even some Scottish commentators who accepted the Guinness bid's slogan **'Bell's Has Lost Its Way'**, although others most emphatically did not. However, even amongst pro-Bell's journalists there seems to have been a general acceptance that Ernest Saunders' move took the Bell's board completely by surprise. The directors, it was suggested, were rather naive not to have seen him coming.

This was untrue. Hints had reached the firm as early as November 1984, when Raymond Miquel was the lunch guest of the City Editor of the *Sunday Telegraph* and was told of a rumour that Guinness was contemplating a bid for Bell's, with Morgan Grenfell as advisers. Miquel was sufficiently concerned to call Morgan Grenfell immediately after the lunch; Christopher Reeves was unavailable but he was able to speak to David Ewart, who said that he had no knowledge of any proposed bid by Guinness for Bell's. Miquel was anxious for Reeves himself to confirm that no bid was in the offing, and asked Ewart to request Reeves to call him should there be any cause for concern. No call was received, which Miquel took to mean that the rumour was unfounded and Morgan Grenfell was not contemplating any action that would run counter to Bell's interests. Ewart represented Morgan Grenfell at the interim results press conference in March 1985, where he was brought up to date with the Wilson Sporting Goods situation and the company's interest in Westin Hotels, negotiations for which had featured largely in Miquel's recent US trip, and which were then at an advanced stage. It was a disappointment for the Bell's team when Wilson was sold to a third party in May, but talks continued with Westin Hotels.

Miquel maintains that Bell's view of its relationship with Morgan

Grenfell was justified, and points out that the bank would have been the obvious choice when it came to fighting off a predator. Ansbacher was a reputable firm and Bell's knew and trusted Patrick Spens, but Morgan Grenfell had more muscle when it came to a fight and far more experience of takeovers. Moreover, its contact with Bell's gave it a knowledge of the company's dealings going back almost two decades, and, he maintains, an important understanding of current structure and strategy, including the recent US negotiations. It was this last point that raised the most concern. Had Morgan Grenfell proved unavailable to Bell's through conflict of interests it would have been inconvenient; to find it on the opposite side was a far more serious matter. Bell's felt it was being asked to join battle against a bank which had been acting as the company's own corporate finance department and whose continuing involvement with Bell's affairs, Miquel reasoned, ought surely disqualify it from acting for a potential purchaser. It was important to raise this objection with the regulatory authorities as soon as possible and for this reason he needed to appoint a new legal team immediately. The two most important advisers in a takeover battle are a company's lawyers and its merchant bank. Guinness had ensured that neither of these were available to Bell's, and although Ansbacher stepped into the breach as far as the merchant bankers were concerned, suitable alternatives were not appointed until several vital weeks into the takeover battle.

Miquel was not due back in Perth for another fortnight, during which time he had a full schedule of calls, including vital meetings with bankers, advisers and others concerning the Westin bid, and a key meeting with Westin's vice-president. He had expected, if all went well, to establish an agreed proposal before his return to the UK, but this was obviously impossible with an unwanted takeover bid hanging over his own firm. The timing of the Guinness offer was unbelievably bad from Bell's point of view. Had the Wilson acquisition gone through in February 1985 then a larger Bell's Group could have been difficult for Guinness to swallow, and now, with Westin close to the handshake stage, the protection that deal promised Bell's had also been thwarted. Guinness, though forced into declaring its bid by a leak that pushed Bell's share price up 103p in three days, still managed to catch its prey at its weakest moment, and with media attention now focused on the company it was possible that other predators would spot the potential of the cash-rich firm with the strong brand and a feeding frenzy would develop. Miquel recognised that even if Bell's did shake off Guinness – which at that stage, unaware of the precision of Guinness's planning, he believed was quite possible – then it would still be vulnerable to opportunists. He took the decision to delay his return to the UK for five days in order to attend meetings in New York. This gave his critics more ammunition, but Miquel's aim during the last few hectic days in the States was to put the Westin acquisition on ice so it could be quickly concluded once Guinness had been repelled, and he was encouraged in this aim by Westin's own continuing enthusiasm for the merger. He therefore fulfilled his immediate obligations in the USA and flew into Heathrow on Wednesday 19 June, going straight to a press conference at the London Hilton at which he confirmed the company's decision to reject the bid. The following day he returned to Scotland and gave a second conference, deriding the Guinness offer and responding to several of Ernest Saunders' particular criticisms. Guinness, he pointed out, with only six per cent of the UK beer market, was criticising Bell's which had 22 per cent of the UK Scotch whisky market. Moreover, Guinness had increased its share of the US imported beer market from 1.6 per cent in 1980 to only 1.7 per cent five years on. The company's performance, he suggested, hardly supported Ernest Saunders' contention that Guinness could do more with the brand than the current management. It was a total, uncompromising rebuttal of the Guinness bid.

Later the same day Bell's official complaint was submitted to the Takeover Panel Executive, requesting that Morgan Grenfell should be barred from acting for Guinness in the light of its long-standing and continuing relationship with Bell's. Both sides had been allowed to make a written submission to the Panel in defence of their position. Bell's gave a detailed description of all Morgan Grenfell's work for the company in recent months and years – Morgan Grenfell's insisted that relations had been effectively severed in February 1982 and that nothing had passed between the two since to preclude it from advising a would-be buyer for Bell's.

As Miquel and his team waited for the Executive's verdict and tried

Bell's executives competing in the North Inch run.

to plan for every outcome, it was business as usual at Bell's. The weekend of 22-23 June happened to be the annual company sports challenge and despite the upheaval of the bid it went ahead as scheduled. Miquel felt it was important in the circumstances that he put in an appearance and played his part in the events, but had to leave early on the Sunday evening to catch the overnight sleeper to London – after repeated refusals he had finally agreed to meet Ernest Saunders there on Tuesday 25th and there were people he needed to see beforehand. As he got up to leave, everyone present rose to their feet and he walked from the room to a standing ovation, the sound of clapping and cheering following him down the corridor to the front door. 'It nearly brought tears to my eyes,' he told a journalist at the time. Messages of support from the staff at Bell's various sites had been arriving at his office ever since his return and it was quite clear that whatever Bell's other shareholders might decide, the employees were solidly behind management in their rejection of the bid.

The Takeover Panel Executive decision came through the following day, Monday 24 June, and it proved a bitter disappointment. Morgan Grenfell was mildly rebuked for its conduct, but there was no penalty or recommendation for further action – in effect, it sanctioned the company's involvement with the Guinness bid. Spens, after consulting Miquel, called for a full hearing of the Takeover Panel and this was arranged for the Wednesday. Meanwhile, as arranged, Miquel met Saunders at the Park Tower Hotel on the Tuesday morning.

The encounter was not a success. Saunders was affable, conciliatory and persuasive; Miquel, accompanied by Henry King in his capacity as a director of Bell's, had no intention of negotiating, and wanted only to make his point and go. Saunders listed the problems his people believed Bell's were suffering, and the benefits of joining forces; Miquel rejected his arguments and said simply that Bell's would fight the unwelcome bid all the way and that if Guinness did take Bell's, he would not come with the package. Saunders smiled and shrugged resignedly, and the meeting was over. It was to be war.

The Guinness case rested largely on its frequently repeated assertion: '**Bell's Has Lost Its Way**', which it used as a headline on all its mailings to Bell's shareholders. Despite the firm's unbroken ten-year history of increasing turnover and profits, Guinness's high-powered consultants kept up a barrage of publicity designed to portray Bell's as a company in decline, whose market lead was being eaten away by the more dynamic approach of rivals like Famous Grouse. They belittled Bell's advertising, ignoring the company's innovative record of PR and sponsorship in building brand image. Barred now by law from using the old slogan 'Guinness is Good for You' in their product advertising, they found that this did not apply to takeover publicity, and it proved a powerful persuader. With the assistance of one of the City's most experienced publicity firms, Broad Street Associates, the Guinness team held out a tempting vision of a revitalised brand with the muscle of an international company behind it, and laid particular stress on Bell's sales record in the US, to which Guinness promised easy access. Knowing how difficult it would be to win over the Press and the institutions to his cause, Ernest Saunders had planned a charm offensive as broad as it was relentless, and every move was monitored daily by Saunders himself and a small committee of strategists, including Saunders' right-hand man, Olivier Roux of Bain Consultants. All statements issued by Bell's to the press were scrutinised by this committee, and anything which touched on the

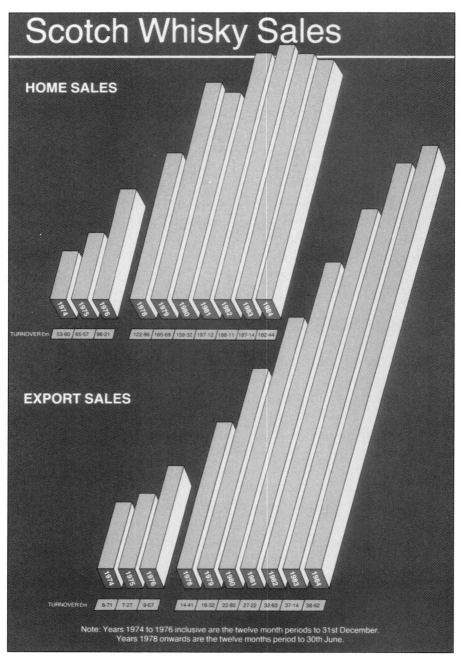

Scotch Whisky Sales

HOME SALES

	1974	1975	1976	1978	1979	1980	1981	1982	1983	1984
TURNOVER £m	53·60	65·57	96·21	122·86	165·69	159·32	187·12	188·11	187·14	182·44

EXPORT SALES

	1974	1975	1976	1978	1979	1980	1981	1982	1983	1984
TURNOVER £m	6·71	7·27	9·67	14·41	18·32	22·85	27·22	32·63	37·14	38·62

Note: Years 1974 to 1976 inclusive are the twelve month periods to 31st December.
Years 1978 onwards are the twelve months period to 30th June.

Sales development over 10 years prior to the takeover by Guinness.

Growth in Group Profit

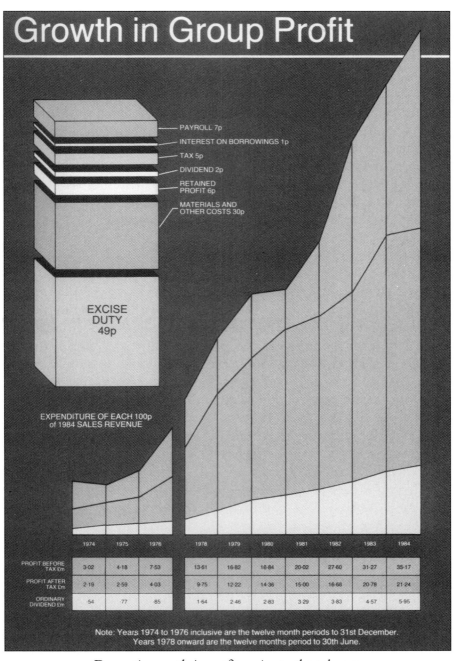

PAYROLL 7p
INTEREST ON BORROWINGS 1p
TAX 5p
DIVIDEND 2p
RETAINED PROFIT 6p
MATERIALS AND OTHER COSTS 30p

EXCISE DUTY 49p

EXPENDITURE OF EACH 100p of 1984 SALES REVENUE

	1974	1975	1976	1978	1979	1980	1981	1982	1983	1984
PROFIT BEFORE TAX £m	3·02	4·18	7·53	13·61	16·82	18·84	20·02	27·60	31·27	35·17
PROFIT AFTER TAX £m	2·19	2·59	4·03	9·75	12·22	14·36	15·00	16·66	20·78	21·24
ORDINARY DIVIDEND £m	·54	·77	·85	1·64	2·46	2·83	3·29	3·83	4·57	5·95

Note: Years 1974 to 1976 inclusive are the twelve month periods to 31st December.
Years 1978 onward are the twelve months period to 30th June.

Dramatic growth in profits prior to the takeover.

company's financial future was immediately pounced upon and reported to the Takeover Panel, which would deem it a profits forecast and demand its withdrawal. Guinness, however, was permitted to continue using **'Bell's Has Lost Its Way'** without any justification.

Meanwhile Miquel was developing a paper with Bell's new lawyers and Ansbacher to present to the full Takeover Panel on Wednesday 26 June, which would indicate the depths of its involvement with Morgan Grenfell over the years to 1985. On the day of judgement Christopher Reeves of Morgan Grenfell, with Saunders sitting beside him on the other side of the 'court', sought to deny that his company had acted for Bell's in any of the occasions listed in Bell's presentation, and asserted that Morgan Grenfell had every right to act for Guinness. Reeves had every reason to be anxious – should Bell's appeal be sustained Morgan Grenfell risked losing not just its sizeable fees, but would also be liable to the other underwriters for an unspecified sum, perhaps as much as £6 million. Miquel, sitting watching events, looked over at the twelve or so bankers sitting in judgement at the large bench at the side of the room and thought that Bell's hundreds of thousands of pounds against Guinness's millions in fees had little chance of winning the day. So it transpired. After just three minutes' deliberation the Panel announced its verdict: Miquel and his team were lectured sharply by the 'court' for wasting the Takeover Panel's time with their submission, and sat like chastened schoolchildren as Morgan Grenfell not only received carte blanche to continue to act for Guinness, but had the Executive's mild rebuke of two days earlier withdrawn into the bargain.

Bell's now needed a heavyweight merchant bank on its side as quickly as possible. The company had no links with any firm save Morgan Grenfell and Ansbacher and the urgency of the situation meant that a single day's delay could damage to its defence. With no time for detailed research Miquel therefore appointed the prestigious firm of S. G. Warburg, trusting that it would bring skill and substance to Bell's defence and that the co-operation of Lord Spens and Ansbacher would supply the insights into Bell's that Warburg lacked. At the time he was unaware that Warburg had worked closely with Morgan Grenfell on the Debenham's takeover only the previous year, a partnership in which Roger Seelig had played a prominent role.

There was, of course, nothing particularly sinister in such a coincidence: all the same, had he realized this, Miquel would undoubtedly have looked elsewhere for assistance. Just hours after Warburg's appointment was announced the formal Guinness offer document was posted to Bell's shareholders and the firm and its advisers discovered exactly what they were up against.

Guinness was just as sensitive as Bell's to the feelings of the Scottish institutions and had set out to woo away Bell's natural advantage in this area from the very earliest days of the bid. Even as Miquel hurried to tidy up matters in the USA Saunders was already playing the Scottish card at a press conference in Edinburgh, making the most of Guinness's Scottish subsidiaries and promising that Bell's under Guinness would retain its Scottish base, management and identity without redundancies, and that the hotels would spearhead a prestigious new international chain. Now the Guinness offer document, like the continuing stream of advertisements in the national press, took up and reinforced these themes. It portrayed Bell's as a stagnant company whose falling share price reflected a lack of firm planning and direction on the part of management. Guinness, claimed the document, would 'revitalise Bell's Scotch Whisky brands in the UK', 'exploit more successfully' the product's export potential, and manage the company's other businesses 'more effectively'. There was an explicit guarantee that not one Bell's employee would lose their job as a result of the takeover, and that their terms and conditions of service would not be adversely affected. Bell's, it assured shareholders, would continue to be managed from Perth as an autonomous company, and even Canning Town Glass could look forward to the benefits of new ownership, since Guinness's own products would provide a substantial new outlet for its bottles. It was a persuasive litany, aimed directly at undermining any clannish instinct for solidarity which might sway Bell's Scottish shareholders. Even so, it might have proved more difficult to win the confidence of the Charlotte Square establishment had the offer not been backed by Noble Grossart, which was Edinburgh's premier merchant bank and a fierce champion of Scottish businesses, and by the law firm of W. & J. Burness whose senior partner Charles Fraser (later Sir Charles) was a respected and influential figure at the very heart of Scottish business and society. Peter Stevenson, a director of Noble Grossart, admitted to the *Scotsman* on Friday 28 June that they expected criticism from Bell's for their involvement with the bid, and reiterated his commitment to independent Scottish firms such as Wm Low and the Macfarlane Group (on whose boards he sat) but insisted that the arguments in favour of the Guinness takeover of Bell's strongly outweighed those against. With the likes of Stevenson, his chief Angus Grossart and Charles Fraser openly supporting the Guinness bid, any hopes Miquel might have cherished that Scotland's great and good would close ranks against the invader were doomed to disappointment.

Quite apart from the look of the thing, Noble Grossart's involvement with the bid had deeper implications for Bell's defence. Miquel, who had little patience with cosy establishment networking, had never paid much attention to who knew whom, but the involvement of figures like Stevenson and Fraser automatically forged links with others whose decisions meant success or failure to Bell's – the institutional investors whose shares Guinness needed. Peter Stevenson, for example, was a friend of Sir Norman Macfarlane (now Lord Macfarlane of Bearsden KT) of the Glasgow-based Macfarlane Group, and a member of his board. Both men were also on the board of Wm Low, and, crucially, Sir Norman was also a non-executive director of General Accident, which held a vital stake in Bell's. In the incestuous world of business such complex relationships are inevitable, but questions would later be raised about the two men's role in GA's eleventh-hour capitulation.

The importance of GA's holding to Bell's cannot be overestimated. When W.G. Farquharson died in 1973 the link between the Gannochy Trust and Bell's was broken, and over the following decade the Trust slowly liquidated its investment in Bell's, offering institutional shareholders the opportunity to build up significant holdings. Some were Scottish; General Accident, whose Perth headquarters lay a stone's throw from Cherrybank, held 12% of the company in 1985, and Scottish Amicable had an important holding; the others were mainly English. While the latter could not be relied on for sympathy, the world of Scottish business and finance was and remains a tight-knit circle centred on Edinburgh's Charlotte Square, where the same names appear on the boards of many institutions, and back in the mid-Eighties there was a distinct feeling of Scottish separateness that manifested itself in support for the successful independent Scottish company. Miquel had never courted the establishment, but even so he might reasonably have expected his Scottish institutionals to line up instinctively with Bell's rather than the London-based international pick & mix that was Guinness plc, and he took some comfort from this supposed advantage.

The force of Guinness's attack was not lost on Bell's board, who were glad when a number of high-profile supporters emerged. One of the most vociferous of these was Perth's local MP, Bill Walker, who had held the Tayside North seat for the Conservatives for some years and understood the contribution Bell's had made, past and present, to the community and the Scottish economy. Walker threw himself into the campaign to keep Bell's independent, expressing his disquiet about the bid to local and national press, and on 2nd July he and three colleagues tabled a motion in the House of Commons which questioned Morgan Grenfell's role in the affair and demanded that the takeover be referred to the Monopolies and Mergers Commission. They secured a 30-minute adjournment debate for 25 July in which Bill Walker was highly critical of the Takeover Panel and suggested that the conduct of Guinness and its advisers might be in breach of City rules. Even after the battle was lost Walker was to remain an active supporter of Bell's, loud in his assertions that the Bell's acquisition had been at best flawed and at worst illegal, and he called repeatedly for the company to be disinvested and restored to independence. When the Guinness/Distillers scandal broke in 1987 he was quick to remind the House of his earlier warnings of 'skulduggery, greed and ministerial incompetence', and treated his fellow MPs to a detailed account of Guinness's flagrant breach of almost every promise in the Bell's offer. Guinness might have taken Bell's, but Bill Walker helped ensure that its methods were exposed to the widest public scrutiny; the firm's conduct in the Bell's and Distiller's takeover would eventually force a much-needed rethink of certain City regulations and practices.

Miquel had made it clear from the first that the Guinness bid was unwelcome, giving telephone interviews to the British papers from his hotel room in Chicago shortly after the news of the offer reached him. His comments were unequivocal – he dismissed the bid as 'extraordinary' and the terms 'inadequate' and questioned the other company's logic, particularly in view of its own recent history. Twenty years of diversification had left Guinness a confused rag-bag of interests, and the company had had to embark on a mammoth rationalisation exercise, selling around 150 companies in three years. The new management's criticism of Bell's, Miquel claimed, betrayed their lack of understanding of the Scotch whisky market. 'You have to decide whether a decade of steady growth is better than one year of growth. What the industry needs is that steady growth, and the depth of management that we possess.' Subsequent interviews found him no less willing to point out the flaws in the Guinness arguments, and once these were formalised in the offer document he and his advisers began work on a more detailed, point-by-point rebuttal of the bid. Bell's first defence document went out to shareholders on Friday 12 July: it rejected any suggestion that Bell's was failing or that Guinness could manage the company better. Much was made of Bell's continuing profitability, which was in sharp contrast to recent results at Guinness. At the same time a submission went to the Office of Fair Trading, requesting that the bid be referred to the Monopolies & Mergers Commission on the grounds that it threatened jobs and was against the public interest. This submission was supported by some of the numerous letters from suppliers, customers and others who saw a successful takeover as a threat. 'Guinness do not have a good track record in job security when swallowing up other companies,' Miquel told the press. 'Too many people – employees and other firms who depend on us for orders – are at risk. We spend £16m per year with Scottish suppliers.' With this in mind Miquel arranged a meeting with Sir Alex Fletcher, a Scot whose position as Parliamentary Under-Secretary of State for Corporate and Consumer Affairs in the Thatcher government made his an obvious target for an appeal on the grounds of potential damage to Scottish industry. Sir Alex, an Edinburgh MP, had visited Bell's head office and knew something of the company, so Miquel believed he could convince him that there was an overwhelming case for the referral of the Guinness bid to the Monopolies and Mergers Commission. He and his advisers were received politely, but it was clear that their arguments did not make the impression they had hoped and that no help was forthcoming in that quarter. Incredibly, in a letter to Bill Walker MP a few weeks later (15 July 1985) Sir Alex even stated that since neither Bell's nor its advisers had ever complained to him about the Takeover Panel's decision to allow Morgan Grenfell to represent Guinness, he had no reason to suppose the decision to have been flawed. One is led to wonder whether the two men attended the same meeting! The general lack of will did nothing for Bell's public interest defence, and unfortunately the Office of Fair Trading was no more swayed by the company's submission than the Takeover Panel had been a few weeks earlier. On Tuesday 23 July the DTI received its report and announced the verdict. There would be no referral – the bid could go ahead.

At this point Guinness still held relatively few Bell's shares and the Board remained optimistic that they could continue to hold Saunders and his people at bay. Miquel had no reason to doubt the support expressed by all his fellow directors and believed their united front remained intact. This was particularly important because speculation in Bell's shares was on the increase and the key institutional investors might well be swayed by the prospect of a high return on their holdings if there was any hint of wavering or disagreement within Bell's board. The previous weekend had seen the Kuwait Investment Office (KIO) purchase almost 5% of the company – 3.8 million shares – at an average price of 270p, despite the fact that the Guinness offer was only worth 225p per share. Analysts suggested the KIO was arbitraging – buying shares at above the bid price in the belief that the bidder will increase its offer before the closing date. This was a risky strategy, since no-one yet knew whether or not the bid would be referred, and Guinness had already passed the first closing date without boosting the terms of its offer. It was even more peculiar in that Kuwait, a Muslim state which observed the Islamic ban on alcohol, was apparently happy for its official London investors to take a stake in a whisky company. Miquel was not the only one who wondered where the KIO's apparent confidence had come from. It had no obvious links with Guinness, but it certainly did with Gleneagles: one director of the KIO had been on the Gleneagles board and close to Peter Tyrie. Still, Tyrie appeared to have put his bitterness at the loss of his firm's independence behind him, and expressed nothing but support for Miquel and his fellow Bell's directors in the fight against Guinness.

Predictably, perhaps, the KIO's involvement was soon in political difficulties. By the end of the following week the papers were quoting the Kuwaiti Finance Minister's orders that the shares be sold immediately and steps be taken to ensure no similar transactions were ever made. Had the shares been sold at this stage to Guinness under the terms of its bid, the offer price of 225p would have meant a loss on the deal of £1.7m for the KIO. In the event they were not sold until 14 August, by which time Guinness had raised it offer to 265p.

Meanwhile Ladbrokes joined the speculators: on 1 August it was reported that the firm, another of Roger Seelig's Morgan Grenfell clients, had bought 3.25% of the company in the hope of negotiating the purchase of Bell's hotels following a successful takeover. When Ladbrokes acquired this interest Miquel arranged a meeting with Cyril Stein, chairman of the company, to see if he could confirm why Ladbrokes was taking an interest and if it intended to make a counter-bid. Stein arranged for the meeting to be held in a private room at Browns Hotel in London at 6.30 p.m. and invited Miquel to dinner. When he arrived Stein was already sitting in his place at the table, but when the waiter arrived to take the order Stein announced that he would not be eating. He was taking his family to the theatre, he said, and they would be arriving in fifteen minutes. Miquel politely declined to order – he hadn't come for dinner – and decided that the whole occasion had been manufactured to make Bell's believe that the Ladbrokes involvement was an honourable one. Stein's family arrived, Miquel was introduced and they all left Brown's together. The meeting was over in less than half an hour.

As the deadline for any increase in the offer drew near Bell's prepared to publish its second defence document. City rules governing takeovers meant this had to be done by midnight on the 39th day of the bid, Monday 5 August, at the latest, and all was proceeding smoothly. Then, on the Monday morning, the market research company that had supplied information on Guinness market share – information important to the defence's arguments – suddenly withdrew permission for Bell's to reproduce its statistics. The refusal was never satisfactorily explained, but it forced Bell's to reprint the document in full and pushed publication back to within an hour of the deadline. The nail-biting last-minute publication attracted close scrutiny, and did have one positive outcome; Guinness had pre-booked large press advertisements for the Tuesday morning in anticipation of the rejection document, and was thus forced into the embarrassing position of rubbishing a defence that had not actually been reported. When the document did come out it retained the defiant tone of its predecessor, rebutting every criticism Guinness had levelled at the firm, but the loss of the Guinness statistics did nothing for its impact. Furthermore, Miquel had insisted that Bell's own figures should be represented honestly and without subterfuge, which meant that the value of the hotels, which could have been used to make profits appear better, was not included. The document concluded:

> Your Board and its financial advisers . . . remain convinced that the Guinness bid seriously undervalues BELL's and has no merit. The Board repeats its advice to you not to accept the bid nor to assist Guinness by selling your BELL's shares.

This was the wording of the advice received by shareholders by post on 6 August.

Early the following day, Wednesday 7th, Guinness announced that it was increasing the value of its bid for Arthur Bell & Sons to the equivalent of 265p per share. Miquel, together with advisers from Ansbacher and Warburg, met immediately to consider Bell's position. A board meeting to consider the new offer was scheduled for the Friday morning, 9 August, and in the meantime Miquel authorised the release of a statement urging Bell's shareholders to take no action over the new offer until the board had met and determined what action to recommend. The statement was an extremely sensitive document, particularly in view of the Guinness habit of pouncing on Bell's releases to quibble about the wording, so every phrase of this particular announcement was agreed by Miquel with Ansbacher and Warburg during a two-hour meeting that morning.

Approving the draft for publication, Miquel felt that cautious optimism was permissible. No major shareholders appeared to have taken the initial Guinness offer in spite of the company's heavyweight campaign, and although the new offer would doubtless bring them a larger stake Miquel considered that a strong Board and a loyal core shareholding might yet see off the bid in spite of all that Guinness could do.

He remained at Ansbacher's offices to talk through strategies in the light of the new offer, and was therefore on hand when a devastating series of blows fell in quick succession. First, at 5.42 p.m., came the news that Ladbroke Group had sold the whole of its 3.25 per cent holding in Bell's to Morgan Grenfell, for 257.4p cash per share. Then, at 6.01 p.m., came the second disaster. Without any warning to his boardroom colleagues Peter Tyrie released a statement indicating that he 'took exception' to that afternoon's statement from Bell's and wished to dissociate himself from it. In fact, he intended to accept the revised Guinness offer, and would recommend others to do the same. A written statement to shareholders would follow unless his colleagues came over to his view when they met at the Friday board meeting. He had, he claimed, already spoken to Miquel about his views, but gave no details, which was understandable since no such conversation had taken place.

Miquel and his advisers were appalled at this development. Boardroom disarray would inevitably weaken the resolve of shareholders and Tyrie's actions would hand Guinness plenty of ammunition for its war of attrition against Bell's board. Sure enough, minutes later Guinness declared that Tyrie's statement was 'further evidence that the report should be accepted by shareholders' and that Bell's board 'should not now further delay recommendation of the offer'. A counter-statement was required, and one was immediately begun. The drafting process was soon interrupted by more unhappy news: at 6.37 p.m. Guinness announced that it had bought 11.27 per cent of Bell's that day, including the Ladbroke stake.

Miquel's own statement was completed and released some twenty minutes later, at 7 p.m. It read:

> The decision of Mr Peter Tyrie to disassociate himself from this morning's holding announcement and his intention to advise recommendation of the Guinness offer is a matter of concern to all Mr Tyrie's colleagues on the Bell's board. They were unaware of Mr Tyrie's

decision to make a unilateral press statement. The board of Bell's is awaiting the full information in relation to the final offer from Guinness which is expected to be published by Friday 9 August before making any further comments on the merits or otherwise of the offer.

Despite the speed of his rebuttal of Tyrie's position, Miquel knew that during a single hour a great deal of damage had been done. The board no longer presented a united face to shareholders and from that moment, despite everything that Bell's could do to prevent it, a Guinness victory seemed almost certain.

Peter Tyrie's sudden defection was ostensibly sparked by the press release put out in the wake of the revised offer, to which he 'took exception'. Although the text advised only that shareholders do nothing, a headline was added: '**Bell's Continues to Reject Guinness's Bid**'. Tyrie claimed that this implied a Board decision for continued rejection, but he had not been party to any such decision and believed that the new offer, which valued Bell's at £364 million, was in the best interests of the company and its shareholders. In fact, as Miquel was soon to discover, Tyrie's apparent conversion was not what it appeared. The truth was that soon after the Guinness bid was announced Tyrie had contacted the Edinburgh finance house of Quayle Munro for advice about his position, and representatives of the firm had regular contact with Guinness and its representatives throughout the takeover period. Quayle Munro had helped form Gleneagles Group and had acted for it during negotiations for the Piccadilly – director Ian Jones knew Tyrie well. Every line of Tyrie's breakaway statement to Bell's shareholders had been vetted by Quayle Munro and its publication costs were subsequently paid by Bell's new owners, Guinness, the company whose bid he was supposed to have been fighting for the past weeks.

The matter of the headline was one of the most crucial and puzzling aspects of the entire affair. Bell's response to the increased offer was obviously vital, hence the considerable effort that went into composing and checking it. The heading '**Bell's Continues to Reject Guinness's Bid**' was most certainly not authorised at the meeting and Miquel finds it inconceivable that the words could have been added to it casually or innocently by some minor functionary between its sanction and publication. It was, he points out, an extraordinarily timely reason for Peter Tyrie's sudden defection, especially when one realises that Tyrie's statement to shareholders had been in preparation for days before the publication of the altered press release. Miquel has never found out who altered the press release, but he is convinced that it was done purely to provide a rather feeble excuse for Tyrie's breaking ranks when he did.

The board met as scheduled on the Friday, but immediately after that meeting there was a second meeting. S.G. Warburg, Bell's merchant bankers, had asked for urgent discussions, and their representatives travelled to Perth to deliver a stark ultimatum. Miquel and the remaining loyal board members remained absolutely opposed to the Guinness bid despite the new offer, but Warburg insisted that they must give up all hope of preserving the company's independence. If the board would not recommend the Guinness offer to shareholders then it must seek a 'white knight' – an alternative purchaser prepared to make an agreed offer for the company. Unless the board announced publicly that it was doing so, then Warburg would cease to advise them and would withdraw completely from the field. It was Hobson's choice; with just two weeks of the offer remaining, the loss of its major merchant bank would have effectively crippled Bell's. With great reluctance Miquel agreed to make the announcement. Whether Guinness won or not, Tyrie's decision to stand alone had ensured that Bell's 160 years as an independent company were over.

The facts behind Tyrie's defection emerged only after the takeover, when a copy of an invoice drawn on Bell's by Quayle Munro was passed to the Press, along with a covering letter from the firm addressed to Olivier Roux at the Guinness head offices in London's Portman Square. The invoice, totalling just under £51,000, had been queried by Shaun Dowling, who described it as 'a hell of a lot', and the matter was referred to Roux who requested a detailed breakdown of charges. This was duly supplied, and it revealed that Tyrie had discussed an approach to Guinness as early as 25 June – the day Miquel had met Ernest Saunders in London – and had secretly been in fairly constant communication thereafter, despite his responsibilities as a Bell's director. There had been frequent liaison with Noble Grossart, Guinness's Scottish merchant bankers, and it was quite clear that rules on confidentiality and disclosure for company directors had been breached on more than one occasion, most notably when the invoice logged a 2-hour meeting with Tyrie on 24 July where Bell's board minutes regarding the Wilson Sporting Goods bid were apparently produced and discussed. According to the invoice Quayle Munro had met with Ernest Saunders at Tyrie's behest on 28 June and had arranged two meetings between Saunders and Tyrie during the takeover period to discuss his position, the first of which took place in London on or before 9 July. Perhaps most telling of all was the evidence that Quayle Munro had been arranging the drafting, printing and distribution of Tyrie's letter to shareholders by 30 June – even though the revised offer would not be made public until the following week. It was quite clear that Tyrie, a director of a firm fighting off a hostile takeover bid, had been aware that the bidder was to increase its offer days before it was officially announced. The invoice laid bare a comprehensive, carefully planned conspiracy of betrayal, and it was obvious from the text that Quayle Munro themselves had not always felt comfortable with events, and nor had the solicitors originally briefed to handle Tyrie's statement, who had declined the work on 5 August and been replaced at the last minute.

The City's takeover code was quite clear about what shareholders should be told. Clause 24.5 included this important piece of information:

> Unless otherwise agreed with the panel, there must be included in every offer document a statement as to whether or not any arrangement or understanding exists between the offerer or any person acting in concert with it and any of the directors, recent directors, shareholders or recent shareholders of the offeree company having any connection with or dependence upon the offer, and full particulars of any such agreement, arrangement or understanding.

It goes without saying that nowhere in any of the documents Guinness released during the bid was there any mention of the fact that Peter Tyrie's advisers Quayle Munro were in constant communication with Guinness representatives, and that the legal costs of Tyrie's independent stand had been underwritten by Noble Grossart, Guinness's merchant bankers, a week before the improved bid allegedly reversed his objections to the takeover. Nor did they go back on their word – Olivier Roux was obviously satisfied with Quayle Munro's explanations, because the original invoice carries a handwritten note from Roux to Dowling, by this time installed at Bell's, stating that the total is a reasonable one and instructing Dowling to pay Quayle Munro without delay. By this time, however, Tyrie was no longer under any illusion that Saunders might sanction a management buyout of the hotels and give him back his company, whatever he might have promised him during the takeover bid. Indeed, it was later alleged that Saunders had never had any intention of so doing, and had actually offered first refusal on them to Scottish & Newcastle weeks beforehand. Tyrie had served his purpose, but as Dowling himself explained to Miquel in the early days after the takeover, Guinness had no future use for a man who had proved capable of such disloyalty, even when they had gained so much from it. Within three months of the takeover he would be out.

Raymond Miquel declares frequently that a good manager is distinguished by his ability to spot an opportunity and make the most of it. To do so, however, you must understand how to lose as well as how to win – and win or lose, you should never look back. This, he believes, is the most important lesson sport has taught him, and it may explain why, when he speaks of the last days of the Guinness takeover, there is no rancour or personal regret but only a shake of the head at the futility of it all. He still drinks Bell's, and will only say: 'I could never change brands.'

Is he still angry about the way things turned out? 'I was never really angry on my own account, although there were certainly a few tears shed on the Friday when we knew it was all over. When I finally left in the January I put it behind me and moved on. It was far worse for the people who stayed, waiting for the inevitable redundancies.' He is realistic, not bitter, about Tyrie. 'He believed they would give him his hotels back if he came in with them. He was wrong, of course. The irony is that I intended to make him managing director of Westin Hotels once the buyout went through.'

There was little realistic chance of finding an alternative bidder so late in the day, but Miquel tried. The statement demanded by Warburg was issued the following Tuesday, 13 August, declaring that Bell's board (excluding Tyrie) and advisers were:

... seeking an alternative offeror to Guinness to allow the business of BELL'S to be run with the right measure of independence so as to ensure the protection of BELL'S brand and its employees and to continue the success of the company.

Guinness, as Miquel had expected, exploited the situation to the full and dismissed the prospect of a white knight, particularly one which could compete with the improved price the company was now offering for Bell's. They seized the opportunity to criticise Bell's board, and when Miquel admitted to a journalist that he would still rather see the company remain independent he was castigated for indecisiveness and irresponsibility. There was some speculation in the press, particularly when the name of Rothmans was mentioned as a potential white knight. No sooner had the reports been published than David Steel MP, (now Lord Steel of Aikwood) leader of the Liberal Party, added his voice to the argument in a statement which received considerable coverage on television and in the Scottish press. His concern was said to stem from the Rothmans connection; the tobacco and brewing giant had strong links with South Africa. A long-standing opponent of that country's regime and a past president of the Anti-Apartheid Movement, David Steel might reasonably be expected to object to such a connection, but he went ahead with an extra-ordinary statement despite Rothmans' assurances that it had decided against any link with Bell's. His comments constituted a direct attack on the Bell's board's handling of the fight, and a direct appeal to Bell's shareholders to accept the Guinness offer. He cited Guinness's recent takeover of the Champneys health resort at Stobo Castle in his own constituency of Tweedale, Ettrick and Lauderdale as an example of the company's excellent management, and advised Bell's shareholders that the firm's best interests lay in immediate acceptance of the Guinness offer, to prevent any further 'maverick manoeuvres' (as he put it) on the board's part.

David Steel's support for Guinness at this critical stage of the process was greatly resented by the Bell's board, and his actions do appear somewhat surprising for a man in his position. He had never visited Bell's and knew practically nothing about the company, but felt able to ignore the entire thrust of its defence and dismiss Miquel's resistance to the initial Guinness offer as 'sentiment'. Bell's directors felt that his words further undermined its efforts to retain the confidence of shareholders, by demonstrating that there was little political will, even amongst Scots MPs, to stand by Bell's in its hour of need. Bill Walker, by contrast, was furious, and later raised hackles in Parliament when he and four colleagues sought to introduce a motion requiring David Steel to justify his involvement in 'selling down the river Scotland's best performing and most profitable independent whisky company'. This in turn provoked a rash of amendments, both sympathetic and otherwise, and Steel and his supporters were stung into a robust denial of any impropriety. Outgunned and out-manoeuvred, frustrated and increasingly isolated in their stand, it is perhaps understandable that Bell's board and loyal shareholders had now begun to assume some kind of hidden agenda whenever the Guinness name cropped up in any connection with the takeover, however small.

The announcement of 13 August effectively put the company on the public auction block and this severely tested the nerve of Bell's institutional shareholders, whose continued support was vital. Miquel knew there was little or no hope of finding another buyer even if he wanted one and embarked on the search with a heavy heart, knowing that it was courting defeat. He did attend the meeting with Rothmans which so concerned David Steel, but the latter's South African connections made them even less acceptable than Guinness and nothing further came of it. He also spoke to Jimmy Gulliver, hoping that Argyll might be able to hold out some hope, but the company whose advances Bell's had spurned during the good times was not inclined to be sympathetic now. (A year or so later Argyll would be thwarted by Guinness in its attempt to buy Distillers, and Gulliver himself would complain furiously about the methods Guinness employed to get what it wanted.) Little hope now remained that the major shareholders would resist the improved offer, and nor did they, although this only became clear during the final moments of the bid. General Accident's board met on Wednesday 14 August to consider the future of its holding in Bell's but it was not until minutes before the deadline of Friday 23 August that the sale of the firm's 12% stake to Guinness was announced. During this final week Miquel had visited GA's investment department, just over the road from

Cherrybank, every day, and on each occasion he was assured that no decision on the disposal of its Bell's holding would be made until the Friday.

The truth was a little less clear-cut. Documents emerged in the aftermath which proved that Peter Stevenson, the Noble Grossart director who had originally explained to the *Scotsman* why the firm had decided to act for Guinness, had written to his friend Sir Norman Macfarlane of GA two days prior to the board meeting and briefed him on the pros and cons of an early acceptance of the Guinness offer. The letter, dated 12 August, makes it clear that Stevenson understood the moral difficulty GA faced; he advised his friend that in transferring the GA's 12% equity to Guinness they 'should not be seen to sell Mr Miquel down the river', and if a white knight did appear before the deadline then an early acceptance would reflect very badly on GA. Nevertheless, he followed this caution with a detailed argument in favour of selling GA's stake to Guinness, with special emphasis on the safeguards promised in Guinness's offer document of no redundancies and operating autonomy at Perth. Sir Norman, who was actually appointed to the Guinness board following the Bell's takeover and eventually became the group's chairman, can have been under no illusions as to how that company had publicly pledged to run its new Scottish acquisition.

Whether Peter Stevenson's points carried any weight with the GA board on 14 August is a matter of speculation. There was certainly no public hint of any decision between that Wednesday and Friday 25 August, hence the constant assurances Miquel received that the investment department was reserving judgement on the matter until the deadline. His gut instinct is that there probably was an agreement in principle to sell GA's holding – it did, after all, represent a handsome profit on the investment – but Guinness expected to gain a majority interest without having to declare the sensitive GA holding. In the event, that twelve per cent proved decisive. Miquel recalls the moment he learned about it.

'I was in the Perth office, and was in constant telephone contact with Patrick Spens at Ansbacher. We'd been talking for a while, following events. It was getting close to the three o'clock deadline and we were starting to think we'd made it – Patrick had even said:

'Raymond, I think we've won,' – and then the announcement came through that Guinness had acquired over 50 per cent of Bell's shares. I knew GA must have decided to sell. It was all over,'

General Accident's conduct, in addition to the matter of the Quayle Munro invoice, would be picked up by the Press in early 1987 in the thick of the Guinness/Distillers scandal, and both were also seized on by the indefatigable Bill Walker, who bombarded Sir Norman with questions and, dissatisfied with the answers he received, aired his concerns once again in Parliament in March 1987. Hansard records that one of his queries concerned the suggestion, allegedly originating with Sir Norman himself, that Ernest Saunders had offered him the chairmanship of Bell's during the takeover bid, but that since Distillers was a major client of his firm he had declined the offer. Was he, Walker also asked, invited by Saunders to join the Guinness board? He certainly did so later. There was a certain irony in all this – the Distillers bid was by now the subject of a DTI investigation, Ernest Saunders had been implicated in an illegal share support scheme by Olivier Roux, and the scandal had also dragged down Lord Spens and his old friend Roger Seelig of Morgan Grenfell. On 15 January 1987 Ernest Saunders would be dismissed from the board of Guinness by the head of the non-executives: Sir Norman Macfarlane.

With the fall of the GA holding the game was up. On Friday 23 August 1985, with a majority of its shares in their hands, Arthur Bell & Sons Ltd became a subsidiary of Guinness plc. Miquel remained chairman and chief executive for a three-month handover period in an endeavour to keep Bell's own management in place, with Shaun Dowling of Guinness and Bell's David Harley as joint managing directors under him, but as he had told Ernest Saunders, he could not contemplate a long-term future with Guinness. On Friday 15 November the licensed trade, which had greeted his reappointment with relief, was disappointed to learn that he would indeed be leaving Bell's at the end of the year. Dowling would become deputy chairman, and Saunders himself would take over the chairman's seat. The promises of continuing autonomy for Bell's now sounded decidedly hollow.

For ten weeks the Guinness campaign had been an irresistible force, but even as the rhetoric subsided the first doubts were setting in. The media, even in Scotland, though divided at first came eventually to a general acceptance of the Guinness line and in the final days of the bid few dissenting voices could be heard. As time passed, though, and it became obvious that Bell's new owner had no intention of honouring its guarantees, there was a certain amount of uneasy shuffling and muttering, particularly amongst the Scottish press and establishment. More than one columnist voiced the opinion that Bell's had been let down badly when it mattered, and this hindsight extended to a more balanced view of Miquel's own record as chairman and chief executive and speculation as to what he would do next. 'He's got the best name in brand building,' admitted one City commentator, 'and if that's where he's going to develop his talents, the City will give him a lot of support.' Another suggested that Miquel should not hesitate to exploit the 'collective contrition' evident in some parts of the Scottish financial community.

Guinness, no longer dependent on the press for support, was too busy tying up the loose ends of the takeover to worry overmuch about any shift in opinion. Tyrie was quickly removed, but those who had assisted the takeover for other reasons were not forgotten. Charles Fraser of W & J Burness, for example, whose early declaration for Guinness had helped undermine Bell's support within the Scottish business establishment, was soon in communication with Saunders regarding the possibility of his firm taking on Bell's legal work. Correspondence between the two makes it clear that the matter had arisen before; a letter from Fraser to Saunders dated 11 November 1985 appears to thank the latter for remembering his intention to put some business his way. On the original there is a handwritten memo from Saunders to Shaun Dowling, directing that Guinness should transfer 'some/all of Bell's routine legal work' to Burness. He also tells Dowling that he would like to appoint Charles Fraser to a non-executive directorship of Bell's if he would accept.

The postscript to Fraser's relationship with Guinness proved a rather unhappy one. Still convinced Guinness had a genuine desire to build Scottish business, he was instrumental as chairman of Morgan Grenfell Scotland in securing Saunders the green light to bid for Distillers, and when Guinness subsequently reneged on its guarantees and demonstrated its utter indifference to Scottish interests, Fraser resigned in what many saw as an embarrassing climbdown. Commentators spoke of his being 'suckered' by Saunders, but to those with first hand experience of Guinness's methods in the Bell's takeover, Saunders' true intentions toward his Scottish acquisitions were never in any doubt.

Bell's, meanwhile, was being absorbed into the Guinness machine and there was no longer any pretence of continued autonomy. A full post-mortem is unnecessary, but the systematic destruction of Scotland's most successful Scotch whisky brand ought surely to make uncomfortable reading for those who declared Bell's best interests would be best served by a merger with Guinness. Miquel himself remains reluctant to dwell on the details of the takeover, but refers questioners to the company's 'progress' over the past ten years or so under the Guinness management.

- **Canning Town Glass** (acquired in 1975 and refurbished at a total cost of more than £11 million, including a new £5.5 million furnace and associated production equipment at the Queenborough factory on the Isle of Sheppey in 1984)
  Both the factory on the Isle of Sheppey and that at Mexborough in Yorkshire were closed, with the loss of over 900 jobs.

- **Pittyvaich Distillery** (built in 1974)
  Closed, with the loss of 20 jobs.

- **Dunfermline Bottling Hall** (built in 1976)
  Closed, with the loss of 180 jobs.

- **Broxburn Cooperage, Bottling and Blending Hall** (built in 1967)
  Closed, with the loss of over 300 jobs.

- **Bladnoch Distillery** (bought in 1983)
  Closed, with the loss of 20 jobs.

- **Cherrybank HQ** (built in 1973)
  Used for some years after the acquisition, although not as an autonomous head office as promised in the Guinness offer, and finally sold to the Bank of Scotland in 1998. Most of Bell's staff there were made redundant.

  Cherrybank's stunning public gardens, the last phase of which was completed after the takeover, are still open to the public although an entrance fee is now payable.

- **Wellington Importers** (bought in February 1984 to achieve access to the US market)
  Sold. No attempt was made to reintroduce and develop the Bell's brand in the US market.

- **Hotels division** (acquired February 1984)
  The Caledonian and North British in Edinburgh were sold, as was the expensively refurbished Piccadilly. No attempt was ever made to use Gleneagles as the spearhead of a large international chain of luxury hotels, as stated in the offer document. Gleneagles' future remains uncertain; it was on the market for a while in 1998 but no buyer was willing to pay the asking price of over £100 million.

- **Towmaster** – sold in 1986 and 200 jobs put in jeopardy.

Sales of the Bell's brand, which in 1985 were running at over five million cases per year worldwide, are a little more than half that a decade later. Indeed, the most recent Diageo annual report (1998) notes a further drop of 300,000 cases in Bell's UK market sales. The 'revitalised' company promised by Ernest Saunders had instead been stripped piece by piece of its independence, its assets and twenty years of careful investment. As an independent the company had invested over £40 million in Scotland in buildings alone and had provided over 2000 badly needed jobs in Scotland and England, to say nothing of the hundreds of others supported through suppliers. Under Guinness and then Diageo it was to become just another brand in a portfolio of many. In just ten years this jewel in the crown of Scottish industry, which it had taken thirty years to build, had been systematically destroyed. Had it been left to continue there is no saying where it might have been today.

Bell's involvement with sponsoring children in the community was soon stopped after the takeover. This included the annual events: the junior tennis tournament; the junior athletics meeting between the home countries; the junior golf tournament; the Outward Bound scholarship programme. They took a long time to develop and little time to close down. The subsidy given to the local Perth tennis club, with its free coaching from Bell's recreation officer for all Perth schools and the facility for Bell's employees, which had been opened with such fanfare by Prince Philip in 1981, was stopped; the facilities were passed back to the club without sponsorship and the members began to struggle once more to maintain the facilities for their own use and that of local schoolchildren.

In addition to stopping these events Bell's new dynamic marketing team under Guinness rushed to copy all its competitors' activities, which included price promotions and the change of the label (five times) and the Bell's blend. The home sales team was amalgamated with salespeople selling other products in the Guinness group. No longer was there a dedicated Bell's sales team. The overseas operation was disbanded as Guinness stopped selling Bell's brand to several foreign markets. The Football Manager of the Year and the Bell's swing ticket club, both highly successful promotions, were also stopped.

'My feeling is,' Miquel says slowly, 'that all the people involved with Saunders and Guinness – the politicians, the businessmen, the bankers, all of them – should look in the mirror and ask themselves, what did they want to achieve by doing it? There was no way it was done for the good of Scottish industry. We have a short-term culture now, where everyone looks for a gap in the market or the chance to make a big fee, and very few people in power are interested in building for the future.' He still muses on Guinness's famous line: '**Bell's Has Lost Its Way**', and believes it might be more accurately applied to a number of people who were party to the takeover.

Almost a year after Miquel's departure the growing rumours of dirty tricks in Guinness's bid for Distillers developed into a criminal investigation and Bell's was back in the headlines again. Miquel was contacted by investigators and travelled to London to make a statement about the role of Saunders, Roux and others in the Bell's takeover, but although the affair was now viewed widely as a precursor to the Guinness-Distillers scandal, it was eclipsed by the far greater scale of the latter.

One interesting experience which came out of the Distillers upheaval was Miquel's subsequent invitation to a Buckingham Palace dinner to discuss takeovers and mergers. It was a formal black-tie occasion hosted by the Duke of Edinburgh, which illustrated the Royal Family's interest and concern over recent events in the City. He was selected as a member of the so-called 'Away Team' of eight, whose members included Michael Howard (then Under-secretary at the

DTI), Sir Jasper Hollom, (the same Chairman of the Takeover Panel who had dismissed Bell's appeal) and Sir Godfrey le Quesne, Chairman of the Monopolies and Mergers Commission. The 'Home Team' facing them included Princess Anne and the Duke of Kent and Miquel recalls that the Princess and her colleagues asked some very searching questions about the rules and practices which had failed to prevent corporate misbehaviour such as that behind the Bell's and Distillers affairs.

As well as the official investigation, the affair also prompted journalists to look again at Ernest Saunders' methods in previous takeovers. Prompted perhaps by Bill Walker, who continued to demand that the Bell's case be re-examined, a few went in search of the company's ex-chairman and asked for his comments. If they expected bitterness they were disappointed. Miquel couldn't ignore what was happening at his old firm but nor would he discuss it: 'I cannot look at what's happening there, I don't want to and I just won't,' he told one persistent reporter. Yes, he confirmed, he still supported Bell's and would always ask for the whisky by name in hotels; yes, he still had an affection for the company in which he had spent most of his working life. Then he drew the conversation firmly round to more important matters: the changes he intended to make in his new role as chairman and chief executive of the Belhaven brewery group.

CHAPTER 6

Belhaven

THE BELHAVEN BREWERY was founded in Dunbar in 1719, although records show brewing and malting on the site as far back as the 13th century. It was bought in the early 1970s by Clydesdale and Commonwealth Hotels and fared reasonably well for a time, but soon ran into difficulty. A stream of chairmen and directors came and went in quick succession – Eric Morley and Sir Fred Pontin had both had a turn in the chairman's seat – and the lack of any consistent strategy had left Belhaven a confused and unprofitable mix of interests, whose share price had tumbled from a high of 300p to around 20p. The major shareholder in 1986 was the Virani Group, run by a family of exiled Ugandan Asians who in only ten years had established a large and successful property empire in the UK. Under the chairmanship of Nazmu Virani the company began to recover; some peripheral activities were sold and efforts were made to consolidate Belhaven's core drinks business. Profits rose to a modestly healthy £1.5m and the share price to 80p, valuing the company at around £20 million, but it was being run at arm's length from London and was still a rag-bag of businesses, some running at a substantial loss, and lacked a sense of purpose. Nonetheless it had an excellent product; Belhaven ales had a good reputation in Scotland and were popular with real ale buffs, and there was every possibility that they might do well in a wider market if given the chance. The company's Spanish hotel, too, was proving to be a profitable concern.

Since leaving Bell's at the end of December 1985 Raymond Miquel had not been idle. He had by his own admission 'tried to retire', attacking his golf handicap and enjoying the novelty of time at home, but a few weeks of relative inactivity and early evening television were more than enough. His chairmanship of the Scottish Sports Council kept him busy, and he also had to make time for his new responsibilities at Glasgow University. Nevertheless he was very soon looking round for a management opportunity which would both suit his skills and offer the same potential for growth and development as Bell's – a tall order, particularly when his severance agreement with Guinness barred him from the Scotch whisky industry for three years. Bruce Johnston, a partner with the accounting firm Arthur Young, who had acted as Bell's auditors for many years, had called Miquel when his departure from Bell's was announced. The two had met twice a year regarding the audited company accounts and, realising he would need a new work base, Johnston offered him the use of spare office space in Arthur Young's Perth premises. From here Miquel dealt with his business correspondence and maintained links with advisers and backers as he searched for the right company. Several possibilities were rejected over the following months, and it was not until the 1986 Commonwealth Games in Edinburgh that a promising candidate appeared. It was there that he was approached by Archie Gibson, joint general manager of the Bank of Scotland, which had been Bell's bank for many years and which performed the same function for the Belhaven Brewery. He outlined Belhaven's circumstances and history, explained that an opening existed at the brewery for a new chairman, and suggested Miquel might be the right person to turn the company around. Miquel did not know Archie Gibson well, but the meeting was a cordial one and he appreciated the information he had been given, which was followed up by a letter from Gibson dated 7 August 1986. It is unusual for clearing bankers to involve themselves in corporate introductions, but Gibson made it clear that he was merely passing on information at the express request of Virani himself, and the financial package he described was certainly generous enough to merit a closer look.

Miquel began to investigate Belhaven. He had talks with Nazmu Virani, chairman of Control Securities which owned Belhaven, who was keen to persuade him to take the company on, and realised this might be the opportunity he had been seeking. Despite the firm's undoubted problems he saw in Belhaven the potential for expansion and success; the brewery business in particular seemed a candidate for his expertise since its history, along with the quality of the product itself, made the Belhaven name ripe for an exercise in brand-building.

He had long regarded brewing as part of a growing leisure market which included restaurants, sport and entertainment. This was the direction in which he had been steering Bell's, and now in Belhaven he saw the potential for another strong Scottish independent company which could pursue the opportunities the Guinness takeover had denied his previous company. Having been run from London for some time it had no overall base in Scotland, but with so many of the firm's key assets there, to say nothing of Miquel's potential backers, a new Scottish Head Office would be far more appropriate.

The deal was supported and brokered by Patrick Spens at Henry Ansbacher & Co., on the strength of Miquel's proposal and Ansbacher's own market knowledge, and involved a number of the latter's large institutional clients. Miquel was to have executive authority and a condition of his involvement was that Belhaven's base should be relocated to Scotland as quickly as possible. When the Viranis relinquished overall control in September 1986 and sold part of their holding the shares were acquired first by Bestwood, a property and investment group with an eye for a bargain, but were snapped up quickly thereafter by Ansbacher's. Other shares were bought on the open market, bringing the Ansbacher consortium's total holding to around 25 per cent, and on Friday 19 September 1986 it was announced that Raymond Miquel had been appointed Belhaven's chairman and chief executive with immediate effect.

The appointment excited a fair amount of interest but during his first weeks Miquel gave little away, although he did make it clear that he had big plans for the company and that a relocation to Scotland would not be long in coming, which delighted the Scottish press. Before long a suitable building had been found in Perth and renovations began to convert the offices, which had once been a fire station and later housed a council recreation department, into Belhaven's new Head Office. He regarded Perth as the ideal spot to work, Miquel explained in one of the many interviews he did at this time, and had always preferred independent regional companies over big London-based conglomerates, believing that more care and thought went into their development. Remembering his unwavering refusal to open a London office for Bell's, thus ensuring that all would-be visitors travelled to Perth to see the company in situ and add their small contribution to the local economy, few doubted that Belhaven would soon be operating in a similar fashion.

Miquel looked at Belhaven from day one with a surgeon's eye, planning to cut away the unprofitable and unrelated pieces of the company and concentrate what remained into three major areas: brewing, leisure and retailing. Disposals would raise some badly-needed cash, but far more was required to develop the firm in the way he wanted, so one of his first important decisions as chairman and chief executive was the proposal of a £13.4 million rights issue. An Extraordinary General Meeting was held on 6th January 1987 to discuss this and other matters, and Miquel held it at Perth's Station Hotel, scene of so many Bell's shareholders' meetings over the previous decades, where an almost festive atmosphere prevailed. Miquel may not be sentimental but he has an appreciation of irony.

Despite an uncertain market the issue was a success, with almost 92% uptake − a remarkable vote of confidence, in view of the blight on the industry and Belhaven's bold expansion plans. Belhaven was now capitalized at £36.5m and Miquel could press ahead with his first wave of innovations. The meeting had also approved a change in the company's name from The Belhaven Brewery Group plc to the more general Belhaven plc, reflecting its intention to diversify. Despite Miquel's interest in the hotel industry he understood that his new company could not support loss-making enterprises, so one of the British hotels was sold within weeks to its tenant and the other two soon followed, leaving only the profitable and developing Belplaya in Torremolinos. Pillings, a specialist licensed trade shopfitters followed quickly, as did the unprofitable Dolamore Holdings (a fine wine merchants) and a chain of off-licences bought from Courage less than two years before.

Meanwhile plans were drawn up for an extensive modernisation of the brewing facilities at Dunbar. The aim was to make it the flagship of the new company and to triple brewing capacity, since Miquel was planning a complete relaunch of the Belhaven Brewery product range and needed to be able to keep up with projected demand. The range comprised a number of draught and bottled ales, and these would now be joined by lager, which the brewery had not previously produced but which was favoured by a growing number of drinkers, particularly in the important 18–30 age group. The most fundamental change was to be the introduction of canned beer for the first time, which Miquel regarded as essential if the firm was to compete realistically in the off-trade. In addition to the increasing production the development plans at Dunbar also incorporated the building of a new reception centre for the licensed trade, with great emphasis to be placed on the brewery's long history and the potential this had in terms of hospitality and public relations. It was the Bell's formula all over again.

The national product relaunch took place in May. All the packaging had been redesigned to achieve a strong brand image across the range, and this was accompanied by a range of drip mats, ashtrays and other pub promotional materials featuring the new company logo and colours (blue and yellow) to complete the package. The appearance of canned beer gave a new dimension to the range, and this was made possible by a reciprocal trading agreement with the Vaux Brewery in Sunderland, which packaged the new product on its own canning lines. The new-look range received a generally favourable response from the trade. The sales function had already been overhauled and placed in the hands of John Rutherford, once Bell's star salesman and winner of the coveted gold publicity award and now appointed by Miquel as Belhaven's regional sales director, and other appointments brought a new air of purpose to the sales team. Initial indications were that the new range was going well and sales would in fact rise by around 20 per cent during Miquel's first year as chairman

By now Miquel made no secret of his ambitions for Belhaven. The revitalised firm was to expand both 'organically' – by the expansion of the brewery business – and by acquisition, with the intention of founding of a national leisure group. The brewing division, which included 41 pubs, would be joined by hotels, clubs, more pubs – perhaps even sports retailers. He retained his conviction that leisure and sport was where the smart money should go, and, as he had done at Bell's, he began to look at linking the Belhaven brand with sport via sponsorship deals. In late July 1987 he announced a sponsorship deal with Dundee United Football Club which saw the Belhaven name displayed on the team's strip, and Miquel let it be known that the company would be looking at sponsorship deals in other sports including golf, subject to the constraints of a limited budget.

When Miquel took over on 17 September 1986 he inherited a number of non-executive directors and associates, but he quickly began to build his own team and within days had appointed Bruce Johnston to Belhaven's board. He was a partner in Arthur Young, the accounting firm, and after the Belhaven announcement Johnston had contacted him. He was considering leaving the company – did Miquel have an opening for him? As Bell's auditing partner he had done a good job in the past, although Miquel admits that he had challenged Johnston regularly about the content and layout of the company accounts. He believes firmly that a manager should never accept advice that cannot be justified when challenged, and over the years has put any number of accountants, lawyers and other expert advisors on the spot, demanding a point-by-point breakdown of the reasoning behind their professional opinion. Johnston had proved equal to past challenges and now appeared genuinely keen to work with Miquel, so an offer was made and a week into Miquel's chairmanship Johnston became his first board appointment. In December they were joined by another familiar face: Henry King, the solicitor who had been non-executive director at Bell's and had proved unable to advise Miquel during the Guinness affair.

The story of Henry King's involvement with Miquel is an interesting one. He was originally introduced to Bell's by a third party, an Australian lawyer Miquel met on a long-haul flight to Hong Kong in 1975. The two had fallen into conversation and Miquel had mentioned his distrust of jargon and secrecy, declaring that he would give a lot to find a good lawyer who was prepared to defend his advice with clear arguments when challenged. The two had exchanged business cards and some months later Miquel was surprised to receive a telephone call from his fellow passenger, who claimed to have found the ideal man for the job. Miquel contacted King and met him in the London office with Geoff Cooper, Bell's finance director. Both were inclined to agree with the Australian's opinion, and by 1979 King was a trusted member of the Bell's board. The Guinness incident had shaken Miquel, since King's inability to advise the company had seriously undermined its defence from the outset, but he was willing to take the incident at face value, respecting the professional ethics which prohibited King from acting. Accepting that the lawyer could not have foreseen the problem when he took on a case for the Saunders family, he was inclined to regard it at best as bad luck, and at worst as further evidence, were any needed, of the extraordinary lengths to which Guinness had gone to ensure its own 'Rough Wooing' met with success. Moreover, the failure to retain King on Bell's board after the takeover suggested to Miquel that there was nothing sinister in the lawyer's involvement with Saunders, although he admits this argument could hardly be applied to Peter Tyrie. Still, King had Miquel's trust, and he had no qualms about inviting the lawyer onto the Belhaven board as a non-executive director to provide the legal perspective. If not precisely a friend, the taciturn King was nevertheless a close acquaintance, and there was no doubting his knowledge and abilities. It seemed hardly likely that circumstances would arise in which he would fail Miquel a second time.

By Christmas the last of the previous directors, the Virani brothers, had left, and with the addition of company secretary Michael Cowie the board was complete. (Cowie, a qualified chartered accountant, joined Belhaven via a recruitment advert, but Miquel had first met him some years previously when he had applied – unsuccessfully on that occasion – for a job at Bell's.) In keeping with his dislike of unnecessary chat Miquel prefers to work with a small board – even at the much larger Bell's there were only seven directors including the chairman himself. Nor does he have much time for those who collect directorships by the sackful and then have to juggle their priorities alongside their divided loyalties. Miquel paid himself and his executives a generous salary, as the 1987 accounts clearly show, and this was supplemented with a directors' share option scheme, but he gave and expected exactly the same level of commitment as had been the case at Bell's, and as at Bell's he did not restrict his incentives to management. An employee share scheme was already on the drawing board and in 1987 details of the proposal would be circulated to shareholders with the company accounts, reflecting Miquel's conviction that employees should have a personal stake in the future success of their company.

Belhaven's preliminary results for the year to March 1987 were published in May of that year, and showed a pre-tax profit of £1.366

million on sales of £16.7 million. Profits were down slightly on the previous year, but turnover was up from just over £13 million and the board felt confident enough to propose an unchanged final dividend of £0.4p per share despite the increase in capital. At the same time shareholders were invited to attend another Extraordinary General Meeting, this time to vote on an ambitious and exciting proposal: Belhaven had made an offer worth £103.5 million for Garfunkel's, a restaurant group based mainly in London and the South-East.

Garfunkel's, which had been floated on the Unlisted Securities Market in 1982 with a capitalisation of just £2 million, was set up by two well-known figures in the restaurant industry: Phillip Kaye and his brother Reggie, who had previously developed the Golden Egg and City Hotels before disposing of them at a large profit. In addition to the Garfunkel's chain itself the company incorporated several other restaurant businesses, notably the Deep Pan Pizza Company and the Biguns Ribs eating houses, and had a total of 90 licensed restaurants. It had been known for some time that Garfunkel's was up for sale and the media had speculated freely about possible suitors, but the agreed Belhaven bid (worth 264p cash per share) took journalists completely by surprise.

In June 1987 Garfunkels was acquired by Belhaven. In effect it was a reverse takeover, since Garfunkels was by far the larger group, and the offer meant that Garfunkels shareholders would end up with 72% of the new company. Nevertheless, Miquel would remain chairman and chief executive; explaining why Garfunkels had not made their own bid for Belhaven, Phillip Kaye said that they 'wouldn't have been able to run it as well as Mr Miquel.' Instead, Kaye and his colleague the Hon. Anthony Montagu, chairman of venture capitalists Abingworth plc which had an important stake in Garfunkels, would join the Belhaven board, a move which was seen to underline the friendly and co-operative nature of the takeover.

The logic behind the bid was one of geography as well as the more obvious shared interests. Garfunkel's, a southern-based business, was ripe for expansion into northern England and Scotland. Belhaven, on the other hand, needed to go nationwide to achieve the sort of expansion Miquel was looking for, and the network of Garfunkel's-owned eating-houses would provide a useful vehicle for the new

Belhaven range. He intended to position Belhaven as a premium brand name, and the Garfunkel's connection would give the company a stepping-stone into the London area and a base from which to build the brand in England.

In April 1988, 10 months after the acquisition of the restaurant chain, Miquel was riding in a London taxi with Phillip Kaye. Suddenly, with no warning, Kaye announced that he believed the company had to sell the Belhaven Brewery; he could not see the logic in the sales development programme that Miquel had for the building of the Belhaven brand. Miquel was stunned. He knew that the forthcoming interim statement, due out in June, would show high costs and low returns at the brewery, but these were an inevitable result of major restructuring and investment and an accepted part of the group's long-term strategy.

To Miquel, Kaye's announcement made no sense at all. The official opening of the refurbished Belhaven Brewery by Princess Anne had taken place only weeks previously, on 24 March. The Princess had unveiled a plaque and toured the brewery, and took away a cheque for

The Princess Royal officially opens the extension to the brewery at Belhaven.

£1500 raised by the workforce for the Save the Children Fund. It had been a red-letter day for the little town of Dunbar and a milestone for the company, and there was an air of excitement and purpose about the brewery, which was running at maximum capacity thanks to the huge injection of cash it had recently received. Now Kaye was proposing to abandon all the work and planning and move the entire operation in a different direction without giving Belhaven a chance to benefit from the £2.4 million it had invested in expanding its brewery operation.

As expected, the June figures showed Garfunkel's performing well, with half-year operating profits of £3.3 million, up almost £0.6 million from the same period the previous year on sales which were up 35% to £24 million. Group profits, however, were up just £0.1 million, due to the high costs of reforming the brewery and selling the new range. This had seen the brewery profits fall from £0.66 million to £0.2 million, but the report stressed that these results were expected and inevitable, due to the monies spent on rebuilding the brewery and expenditure required to build the brand for the future. The packaged market in particular was looking healthier thanks to the advent of canned beer and lager, and the first order had just been received from Japan. The Hotel Belplaya also continued to boost results, and Garfunkel's had taken its first steps into Scotland with the opening of a branch in Edinburgh, one of twelve new restaurants it had opened during a busy year.

This set of results was not received well by the Garfunkel's executives. They clearly felt the brewery was not worth the time and investment necessary to build it as a business, and were therefore at odds with the development strategy favoured by Miquel as chairman. The poor performance of the new Belhaven shares was likewise causing concern. Phillip Kaye asked to meet Miquel on 20 June and announced that he wished to leave the group and take his block of shares (about 16% of the company, including those of Montagu and a particular corporate shareholder) with him. A meeting followed on 29 June, attended by Kaye and Montagu on the one side and Miquel and Henry King on the other; by then Kaye had changed his mind. He still wished to leave, but only if the shares were sold first (Kaye himself had identified a possible buyer, but his terms turned out to be unacceptable to the board). Anxious to preserve continuity at Garfunkel's, Miquel told Kaye he intended to seek new management for the company at once, irrespective of whether the shares were sold or not.

The tensions continued throughout July. Kaye and Montagu sought to force Miquel's resignation, but with the other directors behind him Miquel embarked on a search for new executives for Garfunkel's. Various potential buyers for the company were identified and sounded out, including United Biscuits and Trusthouse Forte, but none proved interested. Miquel was cheered by one piece of advice from Rocco Forte, chairman of THF, when they met: get on with running your company, he was told, and get rid of the Kayes, even if you have to give them a seven-figure sum in compensation. At a board meeting on 11 August Barclays Zoute Wedd, Belhaven's advisers, reported some interest from another potential purchaser, Devonish, but the meeting then stalled over the matter of the Garfunkel's MD. Phillip Kaye appeared to have changed course slightly and appeared more inclined to stay and challenge Miquel. In the end the meeting was adjourned for four days to permit Anthony Montagu to attend.

When it reconvened, on 15 August, it was an extremely stormy affair. Kaye and Montagu were violently opposed to the appointment of a new chief executive and finance director for Garfunkel's, and insisted the board should continue the search for a buyer prepared to offer at least 75p per share. Montagu denounced the proposed new appointments as 'irresponsible' and demanded a delay of at least three months before the question of new management there was even considered. Miquel countered that the recruitment of a Garfunkel's chief executive was of paramount importance to the company's stability, since Phillip Kaye had announced his intention to leave, and that while he would consider selling Belhaven should a good offer come along, he was far more concerned with managing and building the company, as he had been appointed to do. The year's poor results were an expected and necessary part of the development process, he said, and the group's long-term strategy remained unchanged. Backed by Johnston, King and Cowie he won his point, and received authorisation to offer contracts to a new Garfunkel's chief executive and financial director, who had already been identified.

Miquel was due to visit Italy and France in early September 1988. He saw no reason to cancel his trip in the light of the tensions within the board; indeed, if the company was to be sold, it was particularly important to maintain a healthy trading position and seek new contracts. The trip went well but Miquel returned to the UK with new business for the company to learn that in his absence Kaye and Montagu had been persuading the other board members to change sides and were now preparing to vote him out. Bruce Johnston had required Michael Cowie to convene a board meeting before 6 September to consider two resolutions: to postpone the installation of Garfunkel's new management until BZW had exhausted the search for buyers for Belhaven, and to pay the new managing director – who had already been recruited – his agreed salary, but without the appointment actually commencing. On his arrival back in Britain Miquel was contacted in his London hotel by Michael Cowie, who called him on the evening of 14 September to say that he had decided to vote in future with Phillip Kaye, and that an extraordinary board meeting had been arranged for 12 noon on 17 September. Miquel decided not to attend, as he knew there would be a decisive vote in favour of dismissing him. And so it proved, Henry King being the only dissenter. Miquel had been at Belhaven exactly two years to the day. Kaye became chief executive and Bruce Johnston, who had come to Miquel for a job, was appointed as part-time chairman and finance director, two days per week. Plans to sell the firm were dropped and the chief executive-elect of Garfunkel's was told that his services would not, after all, be required. Johnston, the new chairman, wrote to Miquel to tell him he was dismissed and gave him one week to clear out of the office.

The official press statement spoke of a difference of opinion over management and future development, but Phillip Kaye was quick to elaborate. He told the press that plans for the Dunbar brewery had been the cause of the rift; Miquel wanted to make Belhaven lager a top brand in England as he had done with Bell's whisky, and the majority of the board did not believe this was feasible. 'The future of Belhaven is much brighter now that Miquel has left. He is a difficult man,' he said. Reaction to the story was mixed, but it didn't help that the company's results under Miquel looked so uninspiring on paper.

Analysts pointed out that the 55% increase in group profits from
£2.9 million to £4.5 million for the half-year to September 1987 was
largely down to Garfunkel's, which had contributed £3.52 million. By
contrast, brewery profits fell from £665,000 to £217,000 at the mid-
year stage on account of the heavy spending on development.

There were immediate suspicions that Miquel's departure spelt
trouble for those parts of the group unconnected with the restaurants.
Kaye was adamant at the time of the coup, stating to the press that
there were no plans to dispose of the brewery; on the contrary, he said,
they intended to court the trade and expand the business, with
particular emphasis on the acquisition of new pubs. The head office
would remain in Perth, although 'scaled down'. However, change was
already under way. Within one month the board was discussing the
possible sale of the profitable Belplaya and its management company,
Bellhaven SA, as they did not necessarily fit in with the planned
development of the group. Three months later, despite Kaye's talk of
development and growth, the Belhaven Brewery and Bellhaven SA
were sold back to Nazmu Virani and Control Securities.

The Belhaven episode occupied a relatively short time, but it had its
effects on Miquel. Most importantly, he felt he had let down a great
number of small shareholders who had backed him, as he was unable
to see the fruition of all the work he had put in to rebuild the
brewery and develop the branding of its products. The irony is that the
Belhaven Brewery itself, refurbished and enlarged under Miquel, is
continuing to develop and producing good results. In 1998 profits
were £5.8 million, and his belief in Belhaven's future appears to have
been vindicated. Following the sale of the brewery Phillip Kaye
changed the name of the company from Belhaven plc to City Centre
Restaurants and within a few years he had left to start up his own
company again.

Perhaps one of the more disappointing aspects of the affair for
Miquel was the defection of his fellow directors, particularly Bruce
Johnston. Belhaven was Johnston's first foray into the world of harsh
commercial decisions after years in the accountancy profession, and
Miquel knew that he had been uncomfortable with the realities of
turning round a company in financial trouble – as a finance man
Johnston was closely involved with the rationalisation programme to

which Miquel had to subject Belhaven in the first few months. He was also deeply unhappy about Miquel's plan to appoint new management for Garfunkel's, despite Kaye's initial announcement that he wished to leave. Miquel understood the damage that could be caused to the company if it suddenly found itself leaderless and felt that Kaye's talk of leaving, although quickly withdrawn, left him no choice but to proceed with the new appointments. Johnston felt that if Kaye wished to remain at the head of his company then he should do so and in the end, with the prospect of chairmanship before him if Miquel was defeated, he chose to throw his lot in with Kaye.

For Miquel his departure from Belhaven marked a return to the search for a suitable business. In the meantime he learned to ride racehorses and threw himself energetically into his role as chairman of the Scottish Sports Council and his commitments at Glasgow University. He was now at an age when many executives contemplate early retirement, but Miquel had no interest in that particular option. He wanted another company to develop, but he had no intention of beginning another long-term strategy only to have it snatched away for short-term gain. Whatever business he took on this time, he meant to control enough of the equity to ensure that could not happen, and he was prepared to keep looking until the right opportunity came along.

CHAPTER 7

Sporting Challenges and the Community

IN RECENT YEARS the Western world has seen a revolution in our attitude to healthy living. We are far better informed about how our bodies work, and what we should be doing in terms of diet and exercise to keep them working well. Fitness, thanks to the media, is fashionable now. In the States a health club membership has become as vital to one's credibility as an analyst, and even in Britain we have entered the era of the 24-hour gym and the personal trainer. The growth of fitness as a fashion statement, loaded with expensive clothing and accessories, may offend the purist, but in principle we should, as a nation, be healthier than ever before.

In practice, of course, we are nothing of the kind. Obesity is on the increase, not only among adults now but also in children, many of whom enjoy nothing like the freedom to roam of previous generations. Driven to school by busy or anxious parents, many spend their leisure hours at home with videos and computer games rather than out with friends, and although there are schools which do maintain excellent sports facilities, others have been forced to sell their playing fields to developers or have demoted sport within the curriculum as they concentrate on the demands of academic league tables and assessments. Although provision of sporting facilities is far better now than it has ever been, it is a fact that many of us, adults and children alike, never take the opportunity to participate in any kind of sporting activity and never consider the benefits that might arise from doing so.

Ever since he was a boy Raymond Miquel has nursed a passionate love of sport, and while he chose business as a career, the one has always felt the influence of the other. As a teenager he kicked footballs in the back lanes of Glasgow, represented Allan Glen's school at both rowing and tennis, and worked at a snooker hall on weekday evenings to earn cash to fund a game on the Saturday. As a national serviceman in the RAF he found that sport took him from the isolation of the base to any number of matches and competitions, so he made the football, basketball, athletic and tennis teams, playing tennis for Scottish Coastal Command. Returning to Glasgow he began to run with Bellahouston Harriers athletics club, and kept up a punishing training schedule for several years until the demands of career and family made this impossible. Nevertheless, sport continued to play an important part in his life and when he wasn't making news via his business career he was quite likely to do so through his sporting achievements; at 57 he made national headlines when he learned to ride racehorses and applied for a jockey's licence. In his time he has completed the Ben Nevis Race, one of the most extreme challenges an amateur British runner can face, and run in three full marathons, his fastest time a creditable 3 hours 9 minutes. Well into his sixties now, he still keeps trim and fit with a couple of visits to the gym each week and although he is more inclined to play golf these days, he has lost none of his competitive edge.

All sport interests Miquel, but it is as an individual rather than a team member that he has achieved his most notable sporting successes. Running, golf, tennis, horse-racing, even snooker – all involve a direct challenge to the opponent and end with an individual victory. He does enjoy team games too, particularly football, of which he is now a keen and knowledgeable spectator. However, it is probably no coincidence that his own sports of choice, with the exception perhaps of tennis, are those in which an athlete pits his strength and stamina against those of an opponent, even if that opponent is simply his own previous personal best. From a conspicuous overachiever who has always led from the front, one would expect little else.

Miquel's sporting interests have been a constant feature of his business image since he first rose to prominence with Bell's, and commentators have never failed to draw the obvious comparisons with his management style, often describing him as 'aggressive', 'competitive' or 'single-minded'. Miquel himself takes this as a compliment, and points to an early interest in sport as the foundation for much of his lifetime's achievement. It taught him, he says, to set targets for himself, and every success increased his confidence and sense of self-worth. Perhaps more important still, sport taught him how to accept his losses, put them behind him and move on. Arriving as a refugee of sorts in wartime Glasgow, with a French father and an unfamiliar accent, his talent for games certainly made it easier for him to fit in and cushioned him from at least some of the casual cruelties of children. Despite the difficulties and upheavals the war caused his family, and the interruptions to his own education which saw him leave secondary school at 19, he emerged from his teens a confident, energetic young man with great ambition and an appetite for hard work. This, he reckons, is due in no small part to the physical and mental toughness he gained from sport and the self-discipline it taught him, which is why he has always regarded it as an effective tool for the building of character. Throughout his working life he has not only taken advantage of the opportunities he believes sport can offer business but has also devoted time and energy, both as a company executive and as an individual, to the cause of sport and fitness for all.

It was after 1964, once he reached executive level at Bell's, that Miquel had first begun to bring his interest in sport to work with him. The company did have a history of supporting local activities and these included some sport, due mainly to old A.K. Bell's love of games. A firm believer in the benefits of healthy exercise, A.K. was particularly keen on cricket and among his many public benefactions had been the provision of a cricket ground and facilities at Doo'cot Park, near his home at Kincarrathie House. After his death the Gannochy Trust, which took its income from its majority shareholding in Bell's, continued his generous work. One of its most important gifts to Perth had been the Bell's Sports Centre on the North Inch at Perth, which provided some of the best facilities for indoor sport in the district and brought regional, national and sometimes international sporting competitions to the town. The idea for the centre had originated with Miquel; when Farquharson, on behalf of the Gannochy Trust, had mentioned that they were looking for a worthwhile project in Perth, he pointed out the lack of modern sporting facilities in the town and suggested that the community might benefit from a purpose-built sports complex. The Bell's Sports Centre was completed in 1968 and Farquharson had then appointed Miquel as Bell's representative on the Centre's management committee, on account of his particular interest in the matter. The

Prime Minister Edward Heath visits the Bell's Sports Centre shortly after it opened.

company often sponsored events there, particularly where young people were involved.

Miquel has frequently been quoted on the social responsibilities of business and particularly on its local obligations. He sees no conflict between the need to satisfy shareholders and an ethical business stance; indeed, he views the latter as a source of opportunities for a company and lacks patience with those who measure corporate success purely in terms of profits and dividends. 'That's the short-term view. Profits are the bottom line, but they are not the only consideration when you are building for the future.' It was his vision of the possibilities of promotion that underpinned the success of the Bell's brand, but alongside the company's commercial promotions (such as the Football Manager of the Year) Bell's was also generous in its support of some activities which brought it little material benefit aside from general goodwill. It is these that he speaks of as 'social' or 'community' projects, drawing a clear distinction between this kind of activity and the creative, aggressive marketing projects designed to build the brand.

Many of these 'social' activities were local to the Perth area, reflecting the importance Miquel sets on a company's roots in the

community. Others had a wider Scottish interest. A large number had
links with sport and with young people, and were characterised by the
relatively low-key nature of the publicity link with the company. Bell's
gained little direct advantage from sponsoring such activities, since the
participants were mostly barred by reason of their age from the
company's products. Indeed, in its involvement with young people's
events Bell's usually avoided any direct reference to the product at all.
The International Athletics meeting at Gateshead may have been
tagged 'The Bell's Scotch Whisky Games', but for its children's events
the company name only was used, hence 'Bell's Junior Tennis
Tournament of the Highlands'. A cynic might label this as a ploy to
win respectability, but Miquel does not accept this interpretation.
Instead, he points to the scale of Bell's commitment to such activities
and the underlying company culture that supported them, as evidence
that the firm's motives were honest. It is for this reason that Bell's
always negotiated and controlled this type of project itself rather than
leaving the arrangements to an agency, whose main concern would
have been to extract maximum publicity for minimum outlay. Bell's
first concern, he says, was to get things right – to meet the needs of
the sport.

The sponsorship dilemma, sport versus alcohol, was something of
which he was very aware. It was a similar situation which led to his
resignation from the committee at the Bell's Sports Centre in Perth
after only five years. The Centre, which featured three indoor tennis
courts, attracted some fairly prestigious tournaments, and the sponsors
of one such event wished to serve alcoholic drinks at a reception for
top players. The committee was inclined to grant the request but he
was deeply opposed to the idea, feeling that it was opportunistic on
the part of the sponsors and inappropriate for the sports centre. The
potential problems of mixing alcohol with children's events were
carefully avoided in Bell's promotions and he happily admits that this
denied many of the opportunities for hard publicity; this, he explains,
was not the aim. It was about putting something back into the
community.

In 1978 the company was approached by Perth Lawn Tennis Club,
the oldest established such club in Scotland. Once a thriving
enterprise with strong local support – A.K. Bell himself had been one

of its earliest members — it was now in decline, with static membership lists and antiquated facilities which the club could not afford even to maintain, let alone modernise. The initial request was for some whisky to raffle at a fundraising event but Miquel, a keen and skilful tennis player, saw far greater possibilities in the situation. He was struck by the club's potential value as a local amenity, as it was situated in the centre of Perth with easy access by public transport. The site was, however, fairly derelict, with a small wooden clubhouse, and the tennis courts required relaying.

After some discussions Miquel made an offer: if the club would sell the premises and facilities to Bell's for a nominal £1 then Bell's would redevelop it. Memberships would still be available to the public, but responsibility for the running of the club would pass to Bell's and the company's staff and their families would have free access. The committee agreed, but it took some time to persuade the local council to grant planning permission for the work. Some councillors felt the club should move to a site on the outskirts of town, but since Bell's intended to offer use of the facility to local schools it had to remain easily accessible. The point was eventually won and after extensive rebuilding work the old club was transformed into a £250,000 showpiece, with facilities not only for tennis but also squash, snooker and a gym and weights room. Bell's appointed a full-time coach and manager to the new centre; Jimmy MacKechnie was a former British junior tennis champion and a talented tennis coach who had also done a stint as a professional footballer with St Johnston, and had a golf handicap of 3. As Bell's Recreation Officer he not only provided keep-fit classes and coaching for staff and families, but also instructed the classes of local schoolchildren who were allowed to have free use of the courts in the mornings. The emphasis was on encouraging young players, and a new category of junior membership was created and promoted, bringing new life to what had been an ageing and moribund members' list.

The club provided the venue for Bell's regular sporting challenges. The annual weekend of sport was a very popular event and the entire home and overseas sales force was encouraged to participate in the two days of races and contests, with the firm's senior management running alongside them. The weekend included an infamous two-mile

The Duke of Edinburgh visits the Bell's Lawn Tennis Club. Jimmy
MacKechnie, Bell's recreation officer, is on the left.

circuit of the North Inch, during which the assembled sales executives
were usually treated to the view of Raymond Miquel's back
disappearing over the horizon in the direction of the winning line.
Sports fun evenings were also held for the overseas executives when
they returned for their periodic group debriefs, and these were very
successful in promoting team spirit among these hard-working
extraverts and individuals. Most staff made some use of the club, many
on a regular basis. Jimmy MacKechnie kept his own appointments
diary and regularly made himself available at Cherrybank to take
bookings for coaching sessions. Miquel himself arrived at the club at
7.30 each morning for an hour's workout with MacKechnie,
comprising a game of tennis, a run around the North Inch and a
session in the gym, and although there are no figures to support their
assertion both Miquel and MacKechnie were convinced the facility
had a positive effect on Bell's workforce. Miquel himself has always
cited exercise and fitness as the reason for his excellent health – he has

suffered the odd injury but has never taken a day's sick leave from work since joining Bell's in 1956. A fitter workforce is, he believes, a healthier workforce, with associated benefits to the firm.

One of the smaller community-based adult events sponsored by Bell's was the Crieff Highland Gathering, a Highland Games meeting which had been supported in a small way by Bell's for many years. In the early 1980s the company took over sponsorship of the whole event at a cost of £1250, but although there was some small publicity gain the main purpose of the sponsorship was community relations.

During the 1970s and 80s Bell's supported many sporting projects for children and young people which might be classed as 'community' work, amongst which the Bell's Junior Tennis Championships of the Highlands was one of the best known. Originally linked to the main Scottish Highland Tennis Championship and played at Pitlochry, it suffered from a lack of promotion and investment, not least because as a September event it was less popular with players and spectators than the events held at the height of the season. By 1972 it was down to forty entrants and facing the axe. Bell's was approached by tournament referee Jack Braid to see whether the company would take it on, and Miquel agreed on condition the tournament was moved to Perth. The first local venue for the Bell's event was Kinnoull Tennis Club in 1973, but the event grew quickly under its new sponsors, particularly when Bell's sales executives began to call on tennis clubs throughout Scotland to leave details of the event. Entries began to come in from further afield and the organization became progressively more complex. When Bell's opened the refurbished Perth Tennis Club in 1978 the nucleus of the tournament transferred there and Jimmy MacKechnie took over as tournament referee. It continued to develop and grow for a number of years until the Guinness takeover brought it to an abrupt end. By that stage it was the most prestigious junior tennis event in Scotland, contributing most points to individual players' rankings and was immensely popular with young players for the quality of the play and for the organization which was, as Miquel says, like a mini-Wimbledon, with free drinks for each match and complimentary sweat-towels or T-shirts for the competitors. At its peak it attracted nearly 200 competitors in four age groups from under-twelves to under-eighteens, with both singles and doubles

Miquel presents the trophies at the annual Bell's Junior Tennis
Championships at Perth.

events. Over 600 matches had to be played over a week, using courts
in Perth, Kinnoull, Darnhall and Scone, so a minibus service was
provided to move the players around. Entertainment was also laid on;
there was a disco evening for competitors towards the end of the
tournament, and earlier in the week a barbecue in Cherrybank
gardens to which parents were also invited. In 1984 the Bell's Junior
Championships was named Best Tournament of the Year by the
Scottish Lawn Tennis Association. The annual cost of this event was
not excessive – in 1982 it was approximately £7000 – but it proved
one of the flagships of the company's youth sports programme.

Another important annual event was the Bell's Junior Golf
Tournament, a nationwide contest developed with help from Colin
Snape, then chief executive of the PGA. Bell's had a good relationship
with the PGA and sponsored other events for them, including the
biennial PGA challenge match for Club professionals, USA versus
UK. 8500 hopeful young entrants took part in the regional heats of

the Bell's Junior Tournament, all of whom received a Bell's golf towel during their qualifying matches, and the grand final of the contest was played at Gleneagles.

Then there was the Junior Athletics Meeting at the international Meadowbank stadium in Edinburgh. This developed out of the Bell's Whisky Games at Gateshead in 1976, which were held to raise funds for the LVNH charity. The following year Bell's met the Scottish Men's and Women's Athletic Associations to discuss the possibility of a junior athletics meeting, and the first Bell's junior event was held in 1978. It comprised two elements: a 'four nations' contest between England, Scotland, Wales and Ireland, and a number of Open events for young athletes under fifteen or under seventeen. Athletes paraded behind their flags at the start of the event, just as at major events like the Olympics or Commonwealth Games. As always the Bell's sponsorship attracted high-profile sporting personalities to the event and a number of future champions, including Steve Cram, competed at a junior level in the meeting over the years.

In addition to these large, organised sporting events for young people Bell's also funded individual sporting and personal develop-ment via the Outward Bound movement. In 1976 it sponsored an Outward Bound scholarship at Burghead in Morayshire, and by 1982 it financed 66 such places each year, permitting 16-18 year-olds from all over the country to attend three-week residential outdoor sports courses at a purpose-built centre on Loch Eil. Two sail training scholarships for young people were also funded.

Bell's support for the Licensed Trade charities also linked Miquel personally with some of their causes, and although he left the company in 1985 he continued to offer them his support on an individual basis. The tennis courts at the main school at Slough were in a poor state of repair and tennis was not high on the school's agenda. In 1980 Miquel challenged the school's current boys' and girls' tennis champions in order to raise funds for tennis equipment and create an interest in the game at the school. He would play ten games with each and the boy or girl would earn the school £20 a game and £2 for each point they won from him. Miquel would pay £10 per game and £1 per point to the school for every point he won. The result was that he would pay on average £400 to the school per visit for tennis equipment. Many of the children would watch the annual event and a great deal of interest was engendered. The standard of tennis at the school increased tremendously and in the past few years Miquel has played a Buckinghamshire county player. In 1996, after being beaten by the boys' school champion who had just returned from training at the prestigious Bolleteri Tennis Academy in Spain, he decided it was time to hang up his racquet. During the fifteen years he had played in the event he donated approximately £6000 for the school with which several items of equipment had been purchased.

Each year since 1976 the snooker champion of the Licensed Victuallers National Homes has laid down a challenge to Miquel in a three-game match to be held prior to the residents' Christmas party. The match is held at the residents' social centre at Denham which houses an estate of 250 retired licensees' bungalows. A donation is made to the Homes charity on the basis of £20 to the homes for each

Left: Handing over the winnings to the school champions in the annual challenge match at the LV School, Ascot. Right: Equipment purchased from the proceeds.

frame won by the resident and £2 per point, and £10 for the homes for each frame won by Miquel and £1 per point. The match is eagerly awaited by the residents and four weeks prior to Christmas Miquel always receives a reminder. The Homes ends up receiving a cheque for approximately £500 and Miquel is invited to join their Christmas party.

The links between business and sport can run deep. Golf, for instance, may be *de rigeur* in some companies for the ambitious would-be executive, and the subtle and not so subtle point-scoring that goes on in relationships can be suddenly laid bare in a so-called 'friendly' match. During his career Miquel's sporting interests have led him into many business sporting challenges, some public and official, some mere friendly rivalry, and others which perhaps contained a suspicion of both. In 1971, during his first visit to South Africa where Bell's was a leading brand of Scotch whisky, Raymond Miquel was faced with one such challenge. Solly Krammer, who owned several liquor stores in Johannesburg, invited him along with Bell's South African agents and several other guests to a dinner party in his honour. During the meal tennis was mentioned; Krammer stated that he had a tennis court back at his home and challenged him to a midnight game, 'Miquel versus Krammer'. The challenge was accepted and some fairly high wagers were laid on the outcome. Returning to Krammer's house for after-dinner drinks, the party waited whilst the floodlit court was made ready. Miquel changed into his tennis kit but to his surprise his host continued to drink. At the midnight hour a lithe, six-foot twenty-one-year-old bounded into the room, dressed to kill and brandishing a tennis racquet, and it dawned on him that 'Miquel versus Krammer' meant the son, not the father – a typical trick for the competitive South African! With honour now at stake a determined Miquel managed to silence the audience when he beat Krammer Junior seven games to five.

On the same trip he visited Bell's agent in New Zealand, a gentleman named Arthur Hughes who owned the firm which held the Bell's franchise in that country. Hughes had played several games for that country's All Blacks international rugby team in his time and, recognising a fellow sportsman, asked Miquel whether he would care for a challenge game of tennis on the own court in his garden. His first evening in New Zealand they played a singles match which Miquel won very easily. 'Do you play table tennis?' was the next question, and he admitted that he did. The table was already set up in a room in the house, and Miquel again won without too much difficulty. 'Right,' said Arthur Hughes. 'Do you play squash?' 'Yes.' 'OK; we will play at my club at nine tomorrow morning.' The game was accordingly played, and Hughes won easily, 9-1, 9-0, 9-1. 'We never saw the tennis court again,' recalls Miquel, 'but for the five days I was in Auckland I took a thrashing at squash every morning at nine. New Zealanders like to win.'

In June 1981, as a thank-you to six times World Snooker Champion Ray Reardon for his help with the Licensed Victuallers' events over the years, Miquel arranged a three-day weekend sporting challenge (tennis, golf and snooker) at Gleneagles with a points system to determine the overall winner. This event was covered for the Daily Mail by the noted sports writer Ian Wooldridge, who seems to have entered into the gladitorial spirit which characterised the three-day sporting 'house party'. Miquel, he reported gleefully, took the travel-weary Reardon on a four-hour tour of Bell's Perth facilities before the first snooker match, thus exhausting his opponent further and ensuring the autograph-hunters brought on cramp in his cue hand.

'This master-stroke of gamesmanship had the intended result: Reardon did not play well. In fact, he played badly. Deprived of a soothing cigarette in the tiny snooker room at the Perth Tennis Club – Miquel naturally being a paranoiac anti-smoker – he could not overcome the handicaps of deprivation, exhaustion and the 40-point lead he was giving his opponent each frame.

'Miquel forced his way out of several Pythagorean snookers, amazingly won three frames out of the seven and was all for ringing up newspapers all over the world.'

Next morning, however, a refreshed Reardon (handicap 14) launched into the golf with a vengeance and was soon four up.

'Then, according to Wooldridge, began one of the most engaging contests of wills I have ever witnessed in sport. Miquel, handicap 18 and with a swing that reminds you of early Ben Turpin motion pictures, clawed his way back until he was only one down on the elevated 18th tee in front of the lake. Reardon drove and flopped his

The Gladiators seated outside the Gleneagles Hotel.

first ball into the water. He drove a second and hit it unplayably into the mud. He lost the hole, got into the car, arrived back at the snooker hall, made a warm-up break of 87 and then decided to give his opponent and an audience of 23 a demonstration that captains of industry, however dynamic, may occasionally be thwarted.

'He cleared the table with the perfect break of 147.

'You could live 12 lifetimes without ever witnessing it. Two of his shots in achieving it were less improbable than impossible. He smiled like a man who does it every other day and then nipped out to phone his wife. He is 48, has been playing snooker for 40 years and massed 3,049 century breaks. It was his 13th 147.

'Still giving 40 points per frame Reardon wiped Miquel out 7-0 in that session, ending with a break of 92. He then changed into new shirt, shorts and shoes for the tennis and, receiving two games per set and 15 points per game, stood at the far end to take the sort of beating you would expect if John Betjeman were sent into the ring against Larry Holmes.

'They went level into the final game of golf, this time on Gleneagles's Kings Course. While London basked in 80 degrees, the wind in Scotland was a frozen half-gale.

'Reardon smiled as he sank his putt on the 14th green to go four up. It was then that Miquel, representing denigrated British industry, revealed his Glasgow upbringing. Even the caddies, dressed like extras in some Hollywood version of the Book of Job, were urging their men on now and Miquel, pressured like he never is round the boardroom table, won the next three holes.

'It was settled on the final green after three days. Miquel, from 30 feet, missed. Reardon, from eight feet, sank his putt. He won by a single point.

'The handshake was genuinely warm . . . No harder match was played anywhere in British sport at the weekend and none, as in the old days, will go less reported.'

In addition to such competitive sports as these, running has figured largely in Raymond Miquel's life, probably because its simplicity and minimum of equipment makes it an easy sport for a busy man. Indeed, he packed shorts, singlet and running shoes whenever he went away on one of his frequent trips abroad, and had routes mapped out for his early morning run through many of the major cities of the world. The dedication of his few years with Bellahouston Harriers, when he ran up to 100 miles a week, had perforce to be abandoned to career and family, but he remained committed to his morning run, declaring that he reached work full of energy and enthusiasm as a consequence. As a young man he had competed in road races of up to ten miles and had stamina enough to take on extreme challenges like the Ben Nevis race. In 1961 he entered the 22-mile Perth to Dundee walking race and discovered that walking fast was not as easy as running. It was an extremely hot Saturday but he completed the course in 2 hours 29 minutes and came eleventh out of 250 starters. However, golf was out of the question on Sunday as he was unable to walk due to the unusual action required in the race, and he never entered another long-distance walk again, though his serious running career lasted a little longer. It was not until he was in his early fifties that he returned to long-distance events again, with the decision to train for the first of his three full marathons, Glasgow, in September 1983. He completed the course in 3 hours 19 minutes, not only marking a personal milestone but also raising over £2000 in sponsorship for three licensed trade charities. In 1985 he and a team of six from Bell's trained for the Dundee Marathon, this time splitting the proceeds between the children's hospital in Perth and the Tayside

A fine finish at Dundee.

Body Scanner appeal. This race saw Miquel's personal best marathon time of 3 hours 9 minutes. A few months later he completed the London Marathon, his final official marathon run, in 3 hours 35 minutes including time out halfway round for treatment to an injured knee, but he continued to run for pleasure. He ran several half-marathons during the late 1980s and achieved his fastest time at Stirling when he covered the course in 1 hour 28 minutes. As late as October 1991 he completed the Great Scottish Run, a half-marathon, in 1 hour 42 minutes 27 seconds.

His experiences at Bell's and his personal interests made Miquel an earnest advocate of commercial sponsorship of sport and the community and the company's innovative and successful work in the field did not go unnoticed. In September 1979 he was appointed as a Governor of the Sports Aid Foundation, which had been established in 1978 to make grants to rising and successful British sportsmen and women to assist them with their sporting career. Shortly afterwards he was asked to set up a similar organisation in Scotland, which would be called the Scottish Sports Aid Foundation. It would still be allied to the SAF but was to be an independent foundation aimed specifically at the needs of young Scottish athletes of school or college age who were poised on the brink of international success. His plan was to raise sufficient capital from corporate donations to establish a trust fund, the interest on which would be available for grant aid according to the decisions of the governors.

SSAF was set up in 1980. Miquel was founder chairman and initially the governors included Menzies Campbell and the Duke of Hamilton among others. A brochure was produced and circulated amongst likely target firms, and an initial £70,000 was raised from founder members (who donated £5000 each) and associate members, who gave £1000. In its first year of operation the Foundation gave grants of over £6000, all for small sums with a maximum of £250, and these mostly went to pay for travel to competitions or special skills training for athletes.

At first the Foundation was a limited company but in 1983 it became a charitable trust, making its operations more tax-effective and assisting its steady growth. The amount it gave to young people rose year on year, so that by the twentieth year of its operation it had

The award winners at the annual Scottish Sports Aid Foundation Dinner,
March 1998.

awarded grants totalling more than £760,000. An annual awards dinner was instituted to promote the Foundation's work and recognise the achievements of those it assisted. In 1985 Miquel donated a trophy to be presented annually at the dinner with a cheque for £500 to the most promising young Scottish athlete. Over the years many young people supported by the Foundation have gone on to notable success at International, Commonwealth and Olympic level; an excellent result from relatively modest beginnings.

In 1990 he was asked by Eddie Kulukundis, chairman of the Sports Aid Foundation based in London, to chair a committee to look into the establishment of a British Institute of Sport which would be run along similar lines to the Australian Institute of Sport in Canberra. The latter had attracted interest in 1990 when it received some of the credit for Australia's excellent performance in that year's Common-wealth Games. Others on the committee included Derek Casey of the Sports Council, Charles Palmer of the British Olympic Association and Ron Eames, chairman of the CCPR. The British body they proposed would take over responsibility for the existing national sport training centres at Lilleshall, Plas y Brenin, Bisham Abbey and Holme Pierrepoint and raise funds both to improve them and to enable elite British athletes to use them more often and receive scholarships. Too many organisations, it was said, were currently involved in this kind of provision, resulting in duplicated efforts, confusion and wastage. This was several years before the National Lottery's launch in 1995, and although the Foundation for Sport and the Arts had just been established and had allocated money to both the SAF and Sports Council, the Committee decided it was not sufficient to fund the ambitious plans they considered were necessary. However, the subsequent licensing of the National Lottery saw large sums become available for the development of sport and the idea is now back on the agenda.

As a member of the Central Council for Physical Recreation Miquel became involved in that organisation's review of the messy, unregulated area of sports sponsorship in 1984. Commercial support for sport was becoming increasingly important during the 1980s, despite the difficulties of economic recession. Some companies cut back on their sporting links or withdrew from sponsorship altogether, unable to extract sufficient commercial return to justify their investment. This was due in part to a lack of specialist advice in the field; sponsorship deals were negotiated on an individual basis and there was little or no independent guidance for the inexperienced would-be sponsor, or indeed for the sporting organisation anxious for his cash. Instead introductions tended to be made through professional agents or promoters whose fees further reduced the amount of money available to the sport itself. Then, too, controversy began to grow over the role of certain industries in sports sponsorship, in particular the tobacco companies which were increasingly moving into sport as other promotional activities were closed to them. The whole area of commercial support for sport was particularly topical in view of rapid advances in technology, as satellite and cable TV were already beginning to promise an impending explosion in sponsorship opportunities. Sports were increasingly aware that only media coverage would bring them money, and competition was fierce for both.

In 1982 the late Lord Howell, a former Minister for Sport, had embarked on an exhaustive enquiry into sports sponsorship on behalf of the CCPR. His committee reported back in late 1983, and one of its recommendations was for the formation of an association of commercial sports sponsors to promote business support for sport in the UK, particularly amongst the minor and speciality sports which found it most difficult to attract patronage. This prompted the general secretary of the CCPR to arrange two lunch meetings with the CCPR president, HRH the Duke of Edinburgh. The president took the chair to discuss the possibility of forming a sports sponsorship association which would give guidance to members in matters related to sponsorship. A dozen representatives of major companies which sponsored sport were invited and Miquel represented Arthur Bell & Sons at these meetings. The group had welcomed the overall thrust of the Howell Report and the lunch provided an opportunity for its recommendations to be discussed at some length. Three main areas of concern were identified by the president: the recession's effect on sport and the governing bodies' capacity to retrench; alternative sources of sponsorship; and the problems of balancing sponsors' needs with the aims of the governing bodies. Soon after this lunch Miquel was approached by Peter Lawson of the CCPR, who had done a great deal to drive the organisation forward to meet these new challenges, and asked whether Bell's would become a founder member of a proposed new non-profit organisation which was to be named the Institute of Sports Sponsorship, with HRH Prince Philip as its president.

The following year saw much discussion and organisation; the aims and objectives of the proposed ISS were the subject of lengthy debate, as was the format for membership. One major contribution Bell's made was to the corporate image, since the company's own PR people were used to design the logo and the launch pack which went out to the list of potential founder member companies. Despite widespread enthusiasm and sympathy for the project it took a long time to agree the details, but eventually the ISS was officially launched at Buckingham Palace on 27 November 1985, with Raymond Miquel being elected chairman.

The expectations of sponsor and recipient can be entirely unrelated and unless there is mutual understanding the outcome may be unsatisfactory or even disastrous. The ISS was conceived in part to address this issue and as a forum for discussion, but also to lobby on behalf of sports sponsorship issues and to offer its members practical advice on related matters, such as taxation, contracts, media relations and good practice. In this way it should not only make the process of sports sponsorship smoother, but also render it less prone to misinterpretation and failure. Political support came from many MPs with an interest in sporting issues; Miquel recalls that Kate Hoey MP was particularly helpful, as were a number of peers, and the ISS quickly developed friends in both Commons and Lords as it looked to further political measures which would encourage commercial sponsorship of sport. Letters of support for the ISS's objectives were received from Margaret Thatcher, then Prime Minister, and from the other major party leaders.

The ISS has continued to develop its role as the sponsors' voice. It contributes to the debate on topical issues such as sports broadcast rights and tobacco sponsorship and lobbies British and European organisations on its members' behalf. It is involved with the provision of advice and training on sponsorship to sports governing bodies. Since 1995 its annual members' programme has included awards for excellent and effective first-time sponsorship of sport, ensuring recognition for important new sponsorship initiatives.

A non-smoker and moderate drinker himself, Miquel's attitude to the vexed question of the tobacco companies' sponsorship of sport appears surprisingly positive. He reflects the stance taken by the ISS when he states that in his view, if sponsorship money is on offer from a legitimate business source then it can be accepted irrespective of the nature of the business. Indeed, only a couple of years into his chairmanship Miquel found himself before a Select Committee of the House of Commons, giving evidence on behalf of the ISS concerning the issue of tobacco sponsorship of sport, and he made a robust defence of the practice according to his ISS brief and his personal convictions. It is perhaps understandable that Miquel the businessman should look favourably on the subject; more interesting is the fact that Miquel the sportsman has no problem with accepting money from companies whose products are anything but conducive to fitness. 'If that's where a company wants to spend its money,' he says with a shrug, 'then the sport's governing body should take it and be happy.'

Miquel had always had an interest in horseracing, and after leaving Bell's he decided to indulge his enthusiasm and had a number of racehorses based at Bristol. His first horse whetted his appetite and he bought several over the next few years, the most successful of which, Alqirm, won him six races and set a new course record at Salisbury. The Belhaven post, when it came, meant less time to spare for racing but Miquel continued to enjoy his new interest and two of his new horses, Belhaven Bill and Belhaven Special, were named with an eye to promoting his new business. By early 1988 he owned no fewer than five racehorses and made regular visits to the farm of his trainer, Richard Holder, to discuss the animals' progress and future prospects. As usual he was in training and on one occasion he ran around the two-mile paddock four times. When a curious Holder asked why he was running Miquel explained that he intended to raise money for charity by running a half-marathon, to which the trainer replied that if he wanted to travel that kind of distance at his age he should save his legs and use a horse instead. Miquel had never ridden before but the idea stuck, and when he returned to Scotland he contacted a local stable near Perth to arrange a trial riding lesson. The lack of brakes and a steering wheel gave him some pause, but he quickly developed a feel for riding and by August his teacher was confident enough to take him for a trial run round Perth racecourse. He was soon riding out the racehorses at Bristol with the young and aspiring jockeys under the watchful eye of Pat Murphy, Holder's assistant. During this time he would catch the car sleeper train from Edinburgh to Bristol on Friday, ride out three lots of racehorses from 6.30 a.m. Saturday, Sunday and Monday mornings and then drive up to London later that morning for business meetings. He had originally hoped to ride one of his own horses for charity in an amateur race at the Ayr Gold Cup meeting, but by September the storm clouds had broken over Belhaven and there was little time to spare for racing. He refused to abandon the idea, however, and a few months later he was in the news again when he took on the Jockey Club, who refused him a licence on the grounds of his age – he was then 57 – despite the support of his

Riding out at Bristol with Pat Murphy, ex-National Hunt jockey.

racehorse trainer and his exceptional physical fitness, which gave him the constitution of a man half his age. Miquel held out for a medical, arguing that although it was 'policy' not to grant a licence to over-50s there was no actual rule in place, but the Jockey Club remained adamant and for once he had to forgo his ambition. It was a disappointment, but he enjoyed his new-found skill on horseback and maintained his racing links even when business, in the shape of the chairmanship of Lees of Scotland, curtailed the time available for his hobby. He even considered a place on the new British Horse Racing Board when he was approached, but felt unable to commit the necessary time since he was determined to get back into business again.

CHAPTER 8

The Other Side of the Table – the Scottish Sports Council

CONSIDERING HIS KEEN interest in sporting matters and Bell's reputation as a sport-friendly company, it was perhaps inevitable that Miquel's views should be sought on central sports policy and particularly on the benefits of linking sport and industry. He was first invited onto the Scottish Sports Council in November 1983, and represented the Confederation of British Industry (CBI) on the Council for several years, until in September 1987 he was selected to replace the retiring chairman by Malcolm Rifkind, the then Secretary of State for Scotland. This was only a year after he took over at Belhaven, and was a substantial undertaking for a man who was throwing himself into the restructuring and expansion of a business. At the time of his appointment he intended to devote only one day a month to council activities, although subsequent events allowed him to spend more time on the role than he had anticipated.

The SSC had existed for 16 years. Its aims, outlined in its royal charter, were 'fostering the knowledge and practice of sport and physical recreation among the public at large and the provision of facilities therefor'. Funded by the Scottish Education Department to the tune of just over £4.5 million in 1987, it generated an extra £1m by its own activities, and grants were distributed by the council to the 80 or so sports governing bodies. It was, however, a relatively toothless organisation, since its charter gave it no remit to lobby and confined it to advising the Secretary of State on matters within its authority. Miquel took office on November 16 1987, at which time the quango had a membership of 24 and met six times a year. It is fair to say that it was ripe for improvement at the time; in Miquel's words: 'My job was to give the Scottish Sports Council a much higher profile and to streamline it. I wanted to get the members involved more and to put in new financial systems.'

Change was already under way. Miquel had not been idle since his appointment was announced in September, and even before he moved into the Chairman's office Michael Forthsyth MP, the Sports Minister at the Scottish Office, had, at his request, made some dramatic changes to the composition of the Council. The outgoing chairman Peter Heatly — now Sir Peter — whom Miquel knew as a fellow-governor of the Scottish Sports Aid Foundation, was ineligible for reappointment. To his departure were added those of a further nine of the 24 members, who had all been told that they would not be asked to serve a further term. The new Council had just 15 members, six of whom were appointed from amongst the organisation's paid staff in a move designed to streamline the SSC and give it a more competitive edge. Some eyebrows were raised, although few who knew Miquel were surprised that he sought to maximise the SSC's potential and eliminate any cosiness or red tape. The new-look Council was to meet monthly instead of quarterly, and the inclusion of executive officers was intended to produce the most effective link possible between policy and action. Ultimately his hope was that these changes would confirm the Council members, both executive and non-executive, as the ultimate arbiters on strategic direction, priorities and resources.

As chairman of the SSC he was automatically appointed to the Sports Council in London. SSC business occupied a good deal of his attention, but he was also able to leave his mark on the Sports Council too. In particular the move to monthly rather than quarterly meetings which he introduced in Scotland was also adopted by London, as was the reduction in the number of members on the council.

He sat during this time as an inaugural member of the British International Sports Committee (BISC), which was established jointly by the Sports Council, CCPR and British Olympic Committee in 1987 as a forum for the discussion of international issues affecting sport. BISC was an important initiative, the first time that the three principal bodies in British sport had pooled their expertise and resources to boost the country's international influence in sporting matters. Miquel was invited to sit as one of five independent members of the Committee and played an active role in its proceedings for several years.

Early on in his tenure as SSC chairman he decided that there was a pressing need to move the organisation's headquarters. The council had been housed since its inception in cramped and rather inconvenient premises which rambled though several converted terraced houses in Edinburgh's West End. It was difficult for members and visitors to reach by road, car parking was a major problem and rents were high and increasing. Many of the 80-odd sports governing bodies under the Council's aegis were also housed nearby for the sake of convenience and they too found their accommodation unsatisfactory and expensive. A decision was therefore made to relocate the SSC to new premises at South Gyle on the outskirts of the city, and although the developer was at first anxious only to rent the building, a favourable option to purchase soon became available if the Council could find the money. The arguments in favour of the move were strong; it would continue the streamlining and efficiency drive instigated by Miquel on his appointment, and the new site would make the council far more accessible to both members and visitors (both identical reasons for the building of Cherrybank more than a decade previously). Those who questioned the wisdom of such expenditure – the new building would cost almost £3 million – were reassured to learn that one-third was covered by a special Government grant, while the remainder would be recouped in only eight years by the savings on rent from the previous expensive premises. What was more, the SSC would be joined in its new home by 11 of the sports governing bodies who would all gain similar benefits from the move. The point was made, and although Miquel had hoped to gain a larger contribution towards the purchase price from central government, funding arrangements were finally deemed satisfactory and the new headquarters were occupied in January 1989.

One of the Council's main preoccupations during his four-year chairmanship was the promotion of sporting opportunities for the young, which pleased him greatly. He admits to great disappointment, if not surprise, at the cancellation of Bell's various initiatives in this field by its new owners, and therefore gained great satisfaction from his role in Team Sport Scotland, one of the most important initiatives undertaken by the SSC during his time in office.

A detailed study of the current state of sport in Scottish schools was published by the SSC in November 1988 in a report entitled Laying

The Foundations. It revealed a sharp decline in the range and quality of team sports available to young people via the education system. Michael Forsyth was sufficiently concerned at the report's conclusions to ask Miquel to establish a panel, the School-Aged Team Sport Enquiry Group, in February 1989, to consider the current situation and make recommendations. The panel, chaired by Miquel, was made up of fifteen individuals whose collective experience covered most of the major team sports played in Scottish schools; representatives from sports clubs, governing bodies, education authorities, local sports councils and the SSC. Their brief was to research ways of tackling the problems uncovered in the initial report and make recommendations for action.

After an eight-month consultative process the Enquiry Group reported back in October of that year. Its recommendations resulted in the launch of the Team Sport Scotland initiative and brought the SSC an extra £1.2 million from the Scottish Office, paid over three years, to implement a new national development strategy for team sports in school-aged children. The Team Sport Scotland project recognised the importance this type of activity, and through the extra funding it sought to provide it with a wider and more effective base of support.

The money enabled the Council to appoint a co-ordinator for each of the nine major team sports targeted by TSS, all in their twenties and thirties and all with impeccable credentials in their particular sport. The aim was that these co-ordinators should promote opportunities for team-based sport by creating links and local schemes with schools, clubs, local sports councils and local authorities, and organising training and competitive events. Their work was to be monitored by a new Project Director, whose appointment was also made possible by the extra Team Sport Scotland funding.

Team Sport Scotland proved a successful long-term investment for the Scottish Sports Council. The first review in 1994 established that the project, despite limited funding, had made real progress toward its objectives in three years, due in no small measure to the thoroughness and care with which it had been established and the excellence of its staff. The remit of the project was widened to include two more sports and the whole initiative became a permanent, integral part of the Scottish Sports Council's sports development programme.

Although Miquel's principal sporting achievements have been in individual events he has always promoted the importance of teamwork, regarding at as one of the most important learned skills and essential for a successful manager. He has often identified the chief executive's role with that of a team coach, setting policy and providing support for his management teams, and he is uncomfortably aware that the teamwork skills he values are becoming rarer in industry. 'Playing together produces a high level of self-discipline and esprit de corps,' he has been quoted as saying. 'These are not attitudes you can buy.' Children who learn to play effectively in a team will, he believes, carry valuable skills and attitudes through into their adult working lives, and this is a resource which only the most short-sighted would fail to encourage wherever they can. Team Sport Scotland was just beginning its active phase as his time at the Council ended, but his role in developing and shaping the project is obviously a source of quiet satisfaction.

Miquel is positive about the Scottish Sports Council's achievements during his 4-year term of office, and takes pleasure in watching its continuing development a decade later. On the other hand, he would be the first to admit that chairing a quango was a mixed experience for him. The most obvious difficulty lay in the fact that his was a non-executive post, and he was obviously frustrated on occasions at his inability to cut through red tape and get things done. This showed in his contributions to the debate about Scotland's need for national football and athletics stadia, which was galvanised in the early 1990s when Hampden, Scotland's international football stadium and home to the Queen's Park football team, was struggling to find funds for a vital refurbishment. Supporting the Scottish Football Association's call for the upgrading of Hampden, he told one reporter that if the Scottish Office was in a position to fund such a project then the foundations of a new multipurpose international stadium should already be laid. He came into the job in a flurry of controversy, and is fully aware that his reforming zeal was not appreciated by some colleagues; it was not always an easy relationship. However, he does take satisfaction from having guided the SSC through a time of change and development, and left it a leaner and more professional organisation, already reaping the benefits of its restructuring and relocation. The Council's annual grant-in-aid rose appreciably during his tenure, from £4.5 million to a little over £7 million. This reflected the organisation's higher profile and Miquel's vigorous lobbying of central government, and included funding for major projects such as the refurbishment of the National Outdoor Training Centre at Glenmore Lodge, and an incentive scheme to provide matching funds for sporting clubs raising money towards capital projects. He introduced monthly management accounts, just as he has done in all the organisations he has run. Miquel was also responsible for initiating the Council's new corporate image, including a fresh logo and new promotional items, which was launched in October 1989 with the intention of boosting the organisation's public profile. Of particular significance was the sponsor's perspective he could bring to the question of encouraging greater commercial support for sport. 'Ask not what they can do for you,' he explained to the governing bodies of sport seeking sponsorship, 'but what you can do for them.'

Working towards marathons in his fifties brought him back to peak fitness and his chairmanship of the SSC gave him the motivation he needed to remain in condition, sometimes taking drastic action when he felt himself slipping. When his Council duties took him to the Commonwealth Games in New Zealand in 1990 he was concerned about his weight, which had crept up to 12 stone. With a half-marathon coming up he was anxious to get into condition, so regarded the Auckland trip as an opportunity to put matters right. Avoiding all official dinners and taking no formal meals at all, he started each day at around 6.15 a.m. with a five-mile run around the city and then spent the rest of the day supporting the Scottish teams at the various venues. The only food he ate for the entire ten days, he recalls, was the biscuits from the coffee-tray in his hotel room and those he was given when he bought a coffee at one of the venues. The tough regime paid off, and at the end of the Games he returned to Scotland a stone and a half lighter, delighted with the quality of sport he had witnessed but with a somewhat reduced enthusiasm for biscuits.

1991 had been designated the Year of Sport in Scotland, and a series of high-profile events and initiatives was due to culminate in a sports conference and exhibition in Glasgow in the November. Miquel's

With several members of the Scottish Commonwealth Games team in Auckland, 1990.

term of office was due to end on 15 November, but the new Secretary of State for Scotland, Ian Lang, extended it to December 31st to allow him to see the Year of Sport through to its end. When his term of office was completed he reflected on a period which, although very interesting, did not hold the dynamic thrust of commercial activity. It was a case of spending, not making money. The efficient standards required in business are not applicable to quangos, as there is no competition. It was very political, and the chairman was not expected by the executives to interfere with their operation. Although Miquel tried his best to make the operation vibrant, he fought a losing battle; however, the Minister for Sport, Robert Atkins MP, acknowledged his four-year contribution in the warmest terms, and he received further consolation when Alex Cameron, a leading sports writer with the *Daily Record*, wrote of his term in office: 'He will be a hard act to follow.'

CHAPTER 9

Searching for Opportunities

WITHIN A YEAR OF Raymond Miquel's departure from Bell's the Distillers scandal had begun to break and the methods of Saunders and his advisers, now the subject of intense media scrutiny, were casting an unhealthy light on the City and its institutions. The Bell's takeover was naturally re-examined in this light and there grew up a groundswell of opinion, as General Accident had feared, that Miquel and his successful company had been sold down the river. His new start at Belhaven thus attracted considerable and sympathetic media coverage and he was widely depicted, particularly in the Scottish press, as a welcome saviour for the ailing firm. His removal two years later changed this; to some extent Miquel's credibility had suffered and out came the old accusations: he was autocratic and over-ambitious. The press release of 19 September announcing the boardroom changes had been couched in standard noncommittal terms, stating only that it was due to 'a difference of opinion' between Miquel and a majority of Belhaven's board. This dignified reticence was short-lived; within two or three weeks Phillip Kaye was speaking to the media about his erstwhile group chairman, dismissing his plans for the Belhaven brand as an impossible dream and Miquel himself as a difficult and unrealistic man. Miquel kept his own counsel but he was not surprised when the brewery was sold and the new board began, despite earlier denials, to dismantle the Scottish infrastructure.

After the Belhaven fiasco, did he not contemplate giving up? After all, he was approaching his sixtieth year and his career to date had left him with no financial pressure to work. His chairmanship of the Scottish Sports Council had almost three years to run and he had an interesting new challenge in his professor's role; just two of a number of extracurricular projects with which he was still involved. The search for business backing would be a difficult one this time around. Far easier to walk away and enjoy an early retirement. Miquel insists that this was not an option. He couldn't have quit, he says, and he certainly didn't want to retire. Instead he took an office in Perth and embarked on what would be a varied and sometimes difficult three-year search for the right opportunity.

He may not spend time in the greenhouse at home, but gardening is not a bad metaphor for the way Raymond Miquel sets about tending and nurturing a business. The right instincts are needed, as are a certain fatalism, an eye for detail, and plenty of patience. One must know when and where to nourish or starve, train or prune, and above all one must be able to look at a vacant plot and form a clear picture of what it will become, because nothing can be done overnight. Twice now Miquel had seen months and years of patient work and planning swept away when other interests intervened, and both times the stumbling-block had lain in the gap between authority and control. As executive chairman he had the authority to set company policy and direct every aspect of day-to-day operations, but control remained with the shareholders. The most generous service contract in the world cannot keep a chief executive in his post when the owners have decided to remove him. Before he embarked on his search Miquel came to a firm decision – he would look at new projects; he would explore different avenues; he would use his skills and experience where they could best be employed; but he was determined not to take on an executive post again without substantial equity in the company.

There are always business opportunities about, but the process of checking them out can be lengthy and frustrating. It may take days of research to get an accurate portrait of a company, and weeks of negotiations to put together an offer only to have it rejected out of hand. In the weeks immediately following Belhaven Miquel contacted his old friend Lord Spens, intending to use his services in the search for a new company. Patrick Spens was now running Castlecrest Investment, his own corporate finance company, and with his help Miquel investigated Beattie's, a chain of toy retailers based in Hemel Hempstead. Spens had his own problems; he had been forced to leave Ansbacher in January 1987 as the investigation into the Guinness share support scheme gathered pace. He set up Castlecrest two months later and it prospered at first, but in March 1988 he had been arrested and charged over his role in the Guinness affair. Spens would eventually stand in the dock in September 1991 alongside none other than Roger Seelig of Morgan Grenfell in the infamous Guinness Two trial, which was abandoned after four months in February 1992 due to Seelig's ill-health. He did what he could to assist Miquel, but he was under tremendous strain personally and professionally. Miquel continued to look for other openings alone.

One early possibility was Duncan's, a small confectionery firm for which he made an unsuccessful offer with the support of the British Linen Bank. Soon after this he became interested in Edinburgh Crystal which had factories in Edinburgh and Stourbridge and whose owner, Coloroll, was in receivership. He visited Stourbridge for talks with the management and again prepared an offer with the British Linen Bank, but in the end the receiver accepted an in-house bid and there was a management buyout.

His continuing enthusiasm for golf had led him to look at two other interesting opportunities, neither of which proved suitable for long-term involvement but which did give him a new perspective on the sports and leisure industry. One, Kirk Sport Limited, was a very small operation which brought overseas visitors to Scotland on golfing holidays. It had potential as the nucleus of a larger leisure group and Miquel did some preliminary work on the project, even registering a new company name, Bel Sport Limited. His plan was to develop an international group with interests in sporting holidays, travel, conferences, overseas developments and sports retail, all under the Bel Sport banner. He got as far as researching the finance for the deal, but in the end Kirk Sport was just too small an operation to make the theory work and he chose not to pursue the matter further.

Golf Fund Limited was a far larger enterprise altogether. It had been formed by Colin Snape, the chief executive, whom Miquel knew well from his time with the PGA, and was a new company devoted to building and running golf courses which were big business in the 1980s. Miquel joined the board as a non-executive director and consultant on financial matters, working via his Caledonian Consultancy business which he had registered soon after his departure from Belhaven. Golf Fund had attracted serious financial support from the City and already had an executive team. Miquel was a director of the company for almost two years but resigned when he came to the conclusion that there was little possibility of gaining substantial equity or authority in the company.

One project which occupied a considerable amount of time involved a small Glasgow-based firm, Douglas Laing & Co., which produced Scotch whisky for the export and duty-free market. The company owned several brands in a niche market, and had recently undertaken an extensive review which showed, among other things, a need for formal financial planning and reporting and some expert input at board level. The owners, sons of the company's founder, were advised by their consultants to find a non-executive chairman with relevant experience and they wrote to Miquel suggesting he might be interested in taking the post. He worked with Laings for eighteen months, acting as a professional consultant to put management accounts in place and also taking on the role of non-executive chairman. Believing that he could contribute much to the firm from his own experience, he spent a great deal of time with the new finance officer who had been recruited, by Miquel, in response to the recommendations from the consultants' audit, and who proved to be an excellent management accountant and a real asset to the firm. He also worked on development strategies, seeing in the company the potential to develop into a distiller in its own right, and would have liked to have purchased or optioned a portion of the equity, had it been available. Initially this was agreed but the Laing brothers subsequently changed their minds; they wished Laings to remain a family firm and could not offer him the development opportunity he was seeking. In early 1991 he moved on, but wished them well with their business.

One of the more unusual approaches made to him was by a Glasgow merchant bank which wanted to discuss the non-executive chairmanship of Highland Express, an ill-fated attempt to create a new Scottish airline. Miquel was intrigued by the proposal and did visit the young American entrepreneur concerned at the company's smart office suite at Prestwick Airport. Much work had gone into the project, with several routes already negotiated, and Miquel respected the determination of all concerned, but the fact that the company owned only one aeroplane – a 747 recently reconditioned in the Far

East – struck him as a fairly major obstacle, despite assurances that this was a minor detail. He declined the offer with thanks and the post was eventually filled by the late Sir Ian MacGregor. The project received huge media coverage in Scotland and promised great things – Miquel was disappointed but not surprised to hear of Highland Express's failure within a year of the launch.

During this time he had regular contact with venture capitalists, including a London-based company named Apax Partners, and it was early in 1992 that he was introduced by them to one Gordon Manson, a young corporate lawyer who had worked with Touche Ross and who was trying to set up a group of companies under the banner name Claymore Group. Claymore's holdings comprised a pick & mix of assets in Scotland, including two smoked salmon companies. The group's emphasis was on building and development, which interested him, and shares were available to him if he wished to invest. Miquel took legal advice and spent considerable time checking out the company and Gordon Manson. He received excellent reports and in October 1992 he took a financial stake in Claymore – around 20 per cent of the equity – and became non-executive chairman.

When Claymore began to get into difficulties his involvement with the firm rapidly increased and in September 1993 he decided to take the plunge and, along with a partner, acquired the interests of Gordon Manson. Financial difficulties made Claymore a less than attractive proposition for investors but Miquel wanted the core business, Lees of Scotland, which had been acquired by Claymore in February 1993. He had singled it out as a good purchase and attended personally to the negotiations, and although the company was currently struggling he could see a number of basic problems which could be resolved with time and effort, and Lees had an excellent brand name. His co-investor, Klaus Perch-Neilsen, had known of Miquel's success at Bell's and was confident enough to back him if he chose to take Claymore in hand and develop Lees of Scotland as it deserved.

The two acquired 65% of the equity and Miquel became chairman and managing director with a majority shareholding in Claymore in September 1993. After a tortuous period of work and complicated negotiation with the banks Miquel divested it of its unwanted assets – including a nursing home – and arranged workable repayment schedules for the group's considerable debt. Claymore was left with the one core company and changed its name to Lees Group Limited to reflect its new business. Raymond Miquel had assumed control of two dilapidated factories, an anxious workforce, a handful of old-fashioned products and a mountain of outstanding bills.

CHAPTER 10

Business as Usual –
'Lees, Lees, More If You Please'

LEES OF SCOTLAND, based in Coatbridge, was founded in 1931 by
John Justice Lees, who according to the company's mythology
invented the macaroon bar by accident whilst trying to make a
smooth chocolate-covered fondant bar. This sweet confection with its
covering of chocolate and toasted coconut became the nucleus of one
of Scotland's most successful traditional confectionery companies, and
the inspiration for other related products, such as the chocolate-
covered mallow-and-coconut-coated 'snowball', which sold well
throughout the Fifties and early Sixties. 'Lees, Lees, more if you
please!' ran the company's advertising jingle, and for a time the public
did clamour for more. The company fell victim to changing fashions,
however, and its snack products dropped out of favour with consumers
although it did remain the largest maker of meringues in the country,
making own-label meringues for all the major multiples as well as
marketing them under its own Heather Cameron brand name. It
struggled on for years, lacking the will or the resources to relaunch
itself, and eventually lost its independence in 1991 when it was
bought for £4.8m by the Newcastle-based Northumbrian Fine
Foods. There were hopes of improvement under the new owners but
the decline continued; in 1992 it lost £1.6 million and there was no
sign that matters would improve in the foreseeable future. The bank
became restless, and Northumbrian was inclined to cut its losses and
close the firm.

Lees was actually two operations, Lees and Heather Cameron, based
on two separate sites in the town. Both factories had been starved of
investment for years and showed it: the technology was old, the
facilities poor, particularly in the Lees factory which was a converted
cinema. On occasions staff arrived on the shop floor and literally had
to wade through confectionery, which was coming off the production

line faster than the workers could cope. The firm had an old-fashioned image and its products were not competing well in the market, where competitors had kept up with the times far more diligently. Morale was at rock bottom. It was, quite simply, a manager's nightmare, which is possibly what prompted Raymond Miquel to take his original interest in it.

After a period during which he had engaged in little commercial involvement, the acquisition of Lees was quite exciting. The company's situation was desperate – it owed the bank £2.5 million and had a negative balance sheet – and it was obvious that the trouble went much deeper than a simple lack of investment. Miquel immediately set about analysing the problems associated with a failed company, most of which resulted from years of strategic planning failure and unregulated development. There was a lack of reliable financial information regarding the products Lees was producing, but it was established that twenty customers accounted for eighty per cent of the sales, and forty-five per cent of the customers had a turnover of less than £1500 per annum. This was a strong indicator of production problems, since dealing with small orders implies frequent breaks in production and processing. There is also an adverse effect on delivery costs where small, rather than bulk deliveries are made on a regular basis.

The twenty customers which were the mainstay of the company's business were examined in detail. Two of these accounted for £290,000 of Lees' losses the previous year and this had to be rectified. Pricing for products had been reliant on promotion, and the calculations for promotional prices were based on gross profit, there being no accurate way of telling what the net profit per product was. In many instances the promotional price was fed into the computer and at the end of the promotional period the invoice price was not reinstated to its correct level. Unfortunately the company's promotional strategy failed to take account of hidden costs: for example, achieving increased production volume for a promotion frequently involved the staff in overtime, which would not have been figured into the unit price quoted to the customer. Miquel was therefore anxious to bring in management accounts at Lees just as he had done at his previous companies, putting a proper standard costing and budgetary control system in place so the range of products, amounting to 240 separate lines, could be analysed for profitability. He introduced the new system during 1993 and 1994, educating Lees' young financial director in the use of management accounts, and was finally able to audit each individual line to discover its contribution to profit.

This process quickly revealed that almost half Lees' lines made the company little or no money at all. To be accurate, 55 per cent of the company's 240 products produced 99 per cent of the net profit contribution, and once these had been identified Miquel began to discontinue the others. Abandoning loss-making or barely profitable lines, as well as those that sold in relatively small volume but took up disproportionate changeover and production time, he reduced Lees' range from 240 products to just 109. To supplement the new compact range, research began on new products such as cake decorations, children's confectionery and 'snowcakes', and in the longer term these went gradually into development with the aim of filling niches in the high-volume retail market.

Sorting out the workforce problems was a priority for the new management. The unpopular and damaging double shift system was dropped and restructuring began at all levels of staff and management. The complexity of the dual operation meant high staffing levels, and when Miquel took over the company employed 215 people at an annual labour cost of £2.2 million. The rationalisation of the product range, along with other changes, allowed the Lees and Heather Cameron factories to operate with a smaller workforce and by 1997 Lees' employees numbered 132 and labour costs were just over half what they had been four years earlier at £1.2 million. Comprehensive training for the remaining staff was introduced, with the opportunity to gain qualifications where appropriate, and a key aim became multi-skilling, i.e. each employee could do any job in their department. At a senior level Miquel began to assemble and train a new young management team.

With proper financial information coming through, prices were reviewed and standardised. Since they were now based on net rather than gross contribution to profit, they ensured a return on all sales after all costs were taken into account. Promotion and discounting were a fact of life in the competitive food market and Lees continued to operate in this way, but there was no longer an obsession with increasing turnover at any cost as there had been in the past. To get turnover up to the £10 million mark the company had been discounting heavily, using low prices to tempt retailers into so-called 'opportunity buys' where the product is not stocked as standard but bought in as a one-off to sell at a discount, or 'manager's special'. Miquel rationalised this practice and whilst Lees does discount, opportunity buys must make at least a five per cent contribution to profit. There is no more selling at a net loss unless the product is promoted for a period of three to four weeks. In the case of the smaller regular customers, who did stock the product regularly but whose low sales volume made servicing hardly economic, Lees began gently to steer them towards wholesalers, where they could benefit from their supplier's economies of scale and relieve Lees of the high costs of supplying them direct.

Lees' problems were by no means confined to production and sales; the purchasing function was also in disarray. Miquel was aware when he investigated the company that there was no designated purchasing officer, and all buying was done by the two factory directors at Lees and Heather Cameron, in addition to their other duties. The differences in the factories – one made mostly chocolate confectionery, the other meringues – and their geographical separation ensured that there was no attempt at central purchasing and little if any contact between the two factory managers on any aspect of their jobs. Lees' financial problems (and, undoubtedly, the lack of a full-time buyer) had destroyed the company's creditworthiness and negotiation with suppliers was out of the question; it was a case of buying from whoever could be persuaded to sell to them, on whatever terms they were offered. Tankers of chocolate had been known to drive round Coatbridge killing time whilst a cheque was prepared before the driver would relinquish his load. Miquel made plans to centralise the buying function, recruit a full-time purchasing officer and, in the medium to long term, to achieve significant savings on raw materials. First, though, he had to stabilise the company's finances and prepare a schedule for paying off its debts.

Another important area where costs had to be brought under control was Lees' distribution network. The company was involved in a joint venture with its own distribution company, but this was proving far too costly, particularly with the high level of small-scale deliveries to the company's many low-volume customers. One of Miquel's earliest moves was to sell out Lees' interest in this distribution firm and contract the work out, a move which, in conjunction with the increased use of wholesalers, saw distribution costs fall dramatically from £610,000 in 1993 to £473,000 in 1997.

Looking at problems facing Lees as the company struggled to get itself onto an even keel, nobody could argue that Miquel had picked an easy ride. 'I wanted to take on a nightmare and prove to everybody that with the correct approach it could be turned around,' he admits. 'At that time I only had the one personal backer, Klaus Perch-Nielsen, and I was determined to achieve success for him.' To take a failing company and make it pay would be answer enough for those who dismissed him as an opportunist whose only achievements had come in spite of, rather than because of his management style. So long as he had control as well as authority Miquel was convinced he could do what was needed. In addition, he had the challenge of building the Lees brand.

As an astute brand-builder with an eye for an opportunity, one of the reasons for Miquel's initial interest in Lees was his belief that the brand had potential. Lees was, by and large, a Scottish name, although it had achieved a certain level of recognition in the wider UK. Thirty years previously it had been a popular household name in Scotland and affection for its peculiarly Scottish confection, the macaroon bar, had bestowed on Lees' branded products an image of reliability, tradition and family appeal. Time and the company's failing fortunes had diluted the message; the Lees range had little visual coherence and looked old-fashioned and uninviting. Nothing had been done on overall design for years. The factories' packaging technology was outdated and there was no money to replace it, so products were being placed in unattractive and unsuitable packaging which contrasted poorly on the shelf with that of competitors. Cello-packs, for example, were routinely banded together for promotions with cheap sticky tape, a process which not only looked amateurish but which also damaged the fragile confectionery inside.

Despite these drawbacks the Lees brand did retain some positive attributes. It was still widely recognised in Scotland, particularly among those consumers who had known and enjoyed the company's products in childhood, so there was a base of goodwill towards the brand upon which one might build. Its wide range of branded confectionery products, although unwieldy and often unprofitable, had at least kept the Lees name before the public, and the products' place on the shelves of major supermarkets and multiples (Tesco, Safeway, Asda, Somerfield and Woolworth), sometimes at a local and regional level rather than a national one, gave Lees the potential at least for a full UK market presence. Having tackled the immediate problem of looming insolvency and trimmed away the worst loss-making areas, Miquel began to look at the branding issue and push the company and product images upmarket, with the aim of re-establishing the Lees brand and making it synonymous with quality and value.

During his time at Bell's he had found a designer who understood the image he sought for the product and produced the promotional material which Ernest Saunders derided for its simplicity, but which had proved so effective over almost thirty years. Now he was fortunate to find another such artist, a young man named Phil Walker whose own company, Thinx Designs, was based in Newcastle. Walker related to everything Miquel said about the design of packaging. No money was available for material changes, but with his help Miquel overhauled the design of all Lees' packaging to give the range a coherent image, cheerful and appealing, with the emphasis on the quality and Scottish identity of the firm. In addition, he works with Lees' chairman on the creative designs for the company's new products.

When he took over the company a considerable proportion of Lees' production on the chocolate side – 45 per cent of output – was for own-label ranges for the multiples, with no opportunity for branding. On the meringue side the own-label proportion was far higher, at 75 per cent of output. Nor did Lees own its brands. When Miquel took the company on there was not sufficient money available to pay the asking price, so an agreement was reached whereby Northumbrian Fine Foods would keep the brands and Lees would buy them back in due course. Since Lees' bankers – Clydesdale – required its own outstanding monies and interest before any other creditors were paid, it was October 1998 before Lees was in a position

to pay the last instalment to Northumbrian and assume ownership of
its own brand names. By then the proportion of branded chocolate
products had risen to 65 per cent, and two new Lees branded
meringue lines had been introduced for the retail market. The
company's Heather Cameron name remains in use, since it is still well
known in the market for meringue products, but the long-term goal is
to market all the company's branded products under the Lees banner.

The immediate result of the changes, particularly the reduction in
available lines, was a sharp fall in turnover. Sales in 1992 had totalled
more than £9 million but over the next two years of trading they fell
to just £6.7 million. Miquel expected nothing else – he knew
turnover alone was no measure of a company's success. The crucial test
was the firm's profitability, and this showed an immediate improvement. By December 1993 Lees was making a modest profit on its new
rationalised range, and by 1996 profits had risen to £356,000, with
sales figures climbing steadily. The small number of new products that
had been introduced were doing reasonably well, particularly the
kiddies' ranges which traded heavily on the nostalgia the Lees name
evoked in their parents.

The structural and policy changes at Lees reversed the company's
decline and tackled the most pressing problems, but there was little
hope of significant growth until an efficient manufacturing operation
was in place. The two separate sites generated extra costs which could
be eliminated by amalgamating operations in a single factory, but
neither was suitable for expansion. In addition the two factories,
particularly the chocolate factory, required a considerable amount of
financial input to keep up with the increasing demands of hygiene and
safety regulations. Miquel had always intended to look for a new
facility as soon as it became financially possible, and as early as 1994
discussions and research began into the idea of a single-site plant
somewhere in Coatbridge. It proved difficult to secure finance, and it
was not until January 1997 that the company was able to announce its
intentions. Lees and Heather Cameron would be amalgamated, and all
operations moved to a new purpose-built factory on an industrial
estate on the outskirts of the town. A Scottish Office grant for
£400,000 was received and Raymond Miquel had hoped for
co-operation from the County Council for the sake of the local jobs

represented by the company; the previous council had agreed to help, but after local government reorganisation it was a different story. North Lanarkshire Council refused to guarantee the lease, which caused some problems financing the move. However, the new Council did eventually match a grant of £200,000 from the Lanarkshire Development Agency to secure the 150 jobs. This together with the Scottish Office grant amounted to £800,000 towards the £5 million project. Work started on the new factory in November 1997 and without this new facility there would have been no long-term future for Lees in Coatbridge. It had taken three years to get the project off the ground and it is now one of the best purpose-built food factories of its kind, an achievement that will be officially recognised on 19 January 2000 when the Princess Royal will perform the formal opening ceremony. Miquel had taken time planning the facility with his in-house team and several new ideas were built into the factory operation. At the time he announced the new factory development he indicated his intention to float Lees when results justified it, possibly within a few years, although he was adamant – this time he would retain control.

His experiences in starting up again, and in particular his work to set Lees back on its feet, have left Miquel indignant at the inadequacy of business support across the board. The growth and development of successful businesses generates prosperity, but to his mind there is insufficient recognition of this in the policies of the financial sector or the enterprise agencies. He lists a number of obstacles placed in the way of entrepreneurs; for example, he is particularly unimpressed by the overall quality of help and advice available to people trying to build their businesses. Professional consultants do not come cheap, yet in his experience they can often be inexperienced or unsuccessful businessmen, whose qualifications outweigh their practical under-standing of running a company. Many young people starting up in business rely heavily on advice from state-backed enterprise schemes, and while these projects do recognise the importance of supporting the entrepreneur Miquel fears that few can offer the advice and support their clients really need. This problem, coupled with the banks' tendency to levy high rates from such customers, is what turns business-building into such a high-risk, minority activity.

Lees is a case in point. When he took the company on Miquel
knew that it faced pressing practical and financial problems which had
to be addressed urgently if it was to continue trading. It had lost £1.6
million in 1992 and £1.23 million in 1993. Nevertheless, he knew
that a rescue was feasible, and could see what needed to be done. The
two factories constituted a major employer in the town and closure
would mean the loss of jobs which would have a significant effect on
the community. However, when he went looking for practical help to
get the business on its feet, he found it hard to come by. In February
1994 Clydesdale, the company's bankers, insisted on an accountants'
report which they said must be paid for by Lees. It cost £22,000, a
sum the firm could ill afford, and it identified the likely unsecured
exposure to the bank at £2 million, a fact that was already known.
Peat Marwick's report recommended that the bank should increase
the interest charges on its overdraft facility to Lees. It also suggested
the bank take an equity option in the company and consider
arrangement fees and the appointment of the bank's non-executive
director to Lees' board. All very helpful suggestions to the
management at Lees, struggling to keep the company afloat.
Fortunately the bank chose to ignore the report, however the exercise
was costly and utterly fruitless. 'I don't think the bank ever believed
we could pay back the debt and put this company back in profit,'
Miquel asserts. 'We were just a punt – a long shot. I think they just
figured they were going to lose a couple of million pounds no matter
what, so they might as well let us try and redeem the situation. One
would think the money on loan was interest free, but far from it: Lees
paid a considerable amount in bank interest. There was always the
threat that they might just go ahead and close us down.' As things
stand, the bank's decision not to pull the plug on Lees has brought it
its money back with interest. Lees now banks elsewhere, with the
Bank of Scotland.

The new Coatbridge factory finally opened in July 1998 and the
entire workforce moved in under one roof. There were implications
for the company's finances and it is early days yet, but the company's
future at last looks promising. Sales are up and growing. Most of the
multiples are stocking Lees products; the all-important English market
is opening to them little by little. The net profit for Lees Group Ltd in

1998 was £556,000 which has enabled the company to reduce its very substantial debt, and if the trend continues then the company's future in the new millennium looks bright. There have been enormous problems in modernising the company, and even though the new premises are now open there are still difficulties to overcome. Rising profits have finally enabled the purchase of a new machine which will box the products, increasing the shelf appeal, and Miquel hopes this will pay for itself in increased sales and less damage to the new, sturdily packaged goods. Turning a company round can be slow, frustrating work but it is something Miquel thrives on.

The success of a company can be gauged by the quality of its senior management. In rebuilding Lees the first two years was spent recruiting and building the management team. Apart from Miquel, Lees has a young board of executive directors with an average age of 35 years. The new purchasing officer appointed in 1995 has now progressed to become the administration director, and he is joined by the finance director and two directors associated with sales. Salespeople with the correct attitudes and abilities are always the most difficult to find, but after several changes Miquel has appointed a sales director and a sales and marketing director with qualities he is certain will ensure the growth in sales of the Lees products. The company has recently appointed a new production director to take on the increased responsibilities associated with the new factory development. Teamwork is an essential part of Miquel's management philosophy and having a team that can work well together is vitally important. Currently in Lees he feels he has achieved this objective and the young team of directors are all shareholders in the company.

It is hoped that an employee share scheme can be introduced in 1999. In both Bell's and Belhaven a free share scheme for all employees was established. In Lees shares have been purchased by an Employee Share Trust and if the share scheme is approved it will enable free shares to be allocated to all full-time employees on an annual basis, with everybody in the company receiving the same number of shares each year.

Throughout his career a criticism regularly levelled at Miquel *qua* manager has been that he cannot operate 'hands off'. Although he is remembered at the Scottish Sports Council as a builder and reformer, there were many who found it difficult to accept such a high level of involvement in a supposedly non-executive role.

Miquel prefers his companies to be defined by their policies and objectives. Where these are fully and clearly understood by all executives then individuals can be given freedom to operate within a defined area, with any policy decision referred back to the executive chairman. Frequent discussion and consultation are essential so that executives understand what is happening outside their own sphere of influence and the executive chairman has an overview of the entire company's operations. If this is interpreted as a 'one-man band' approach, he appears to say, then so be it. He prefers to define it as leadership.

Raymond Miquel builds companies because he wants to and because he can, in much the same way that he has ridden racehorses, or run up mountains, or completed marathons ahead of men half his age. Perhaps some of his affection for his adopted country can be explained in terms of character, since he possesses an abundance of that peculiar stubborn single-mindedness that Scots have celebrated for centuries as perhaps the greatest of their national virtues. Many have found him abrasive and awkward; others describe him as straightforward and almost obsessively even-handed. He has been variously criticised for lacking the usual businessman's guile, or for having too much of it. Whatever else may be true, it is undoubtedly the competitor in him that has kept him going, absorbing success and failure alike, attention always moving away from today's result to the next target, confident in his ability to cope with whatever comes his way. Business, in short, as usual.

The Miquel Way

'I studied all aspects of business, but I have to say that the marketing function, and particularly brand-building, have always attracted me far more than the day-to-day details of management. I don't think I would have enjoyed just managing a company.'

'I'm not ruthless or aggressive, but I am competitive: I always have been. I learned early on that winning beats losing.'

'It's very important to learn to win and lose, and accept disappointment and criticism. People who don't understand what you're doing will always be ready to criticise you.'

'I like working with a young team. Their attitudes are less fixed than those of older people. They don't think they know everything, and they can be trained to do things the way you want them done.'

'The key to motivation is the satisfaction of seeing things happen. If you can make things happen, people will tend to want to get involved.'

'There's a lot said about delegation in industry, but I believe a manager needs to understand the project and the subject inside out, and give the job in hand his or her undivided attention.'

'You get a great deal of satisfaction in building a company. It becomes your lifestyle; it becomes your hobby. It means there's always something interesting going on.'

'If you look at businesses that have failed, its the pyramid style of management that invariably gets them into trouble. It leads to secrecy and bad management practice – that's why I prefer to get people working in teams.'

'Teamwork is definitely lacking in industry today. The gulf between shop-floor and management is still far too wide and that breeds selfish attitudes. People too often work for themselves and not for the company.'

'If people are fit and healthy they do their job so much better.'

'Playing together produces a high level of self-discipline and an *esprit de corps* among the staff. These are not attitudes you can buy.'

'I see no conflict between the needs of the shareholders and the wider obligation business owes the community. Profits are the bottom line, but they are not the only consideration when you are building for the future.'